FIDEL CASTRO

Recent Titles in Greenwood Biographies

FIDEL CASTRO

A Biography

Thomas M. Leonard

GREENWOOD BIOGRAPHIES

GREENWOOD PRESS
WESTPORT, CONNECTICUT · LONDON

β CASTRO

Library of Congress Cataloging-in-Publication Data

Leonard, Thomas M., 1937–
   Fidel Castro : a biography / Thomas M. Leonard.—1st ed.
     p. cm.—(Greenwood biograpies, ISSN 1540–4900)
   Includes bibliographical references and index.
   ISBN 0–313–32301–1 (alk. paper)
   1. Castro, Fidel, 1926– 2. Cuba—History—1933–1959. 3. Cuba—History—1959–
4. Heads of state—Cuba—Biography. 1. Title. II. Series.
F1788.22.C3L46   2004
972.9106′4′092—dc22   2004005995

British Library Cataloguing in Publication Data is available.

Library of Congress Catalog Card Number: 2004005995
ISBN: 0–313–32301–1
ISSN: 1540–4900

First published in 2004

Greenwood Press, 88 Post Road West, Westport, CT 06881
An imprint of Greenwood Publishing Group, Inc.
www.greenwood.com

Printed in the United States of America

The paper used in this book complies with the
Permanent Paper Standard issued by the National
Information Standards Organization (Z39.48–1984).

10 9 8 7 6 5 4 3 2 1

For My Students

CONTENTS

Photo essay follows page 70

SERIES FOREWORD

In response to high school and public library needs, Greenwood developed this distinguished series of full-length biographies specifically for student use. Prepared by field experts and professionals, these engaging biographies are tailored for high school students who need challenging yet accessible biographies. Ideal for secondary school assignments, the length, format, and subject areas are designed to meet educators' requirements and students' interests.

Greenwood offers an extensive selection of biographies spanning all curriculum related subject areas including social studies, the sciences, literature and the arts, history and politics, as well as popular culture, covering public figures and famous personalities from all time periods and backgrounds, both historic and contemporary, who have made an impact on American and/or world culture. Greenwood biographies were chosen based on comprehensive feedback from librarians and educators. Consideration was given to both curriculum relevance and inherent interest. The result is an intriguing mix of the well known and the unexpected, the saints and the sinners from long-ago history and contemporary pop culture. Readers will find a wide array of subject choices from fascinating crime figures like Al Capone to inspiring pioneers like Margaret Mead, from the greatest minds of our time like Stephen Hawking to the most amazing success stories of our day like J. K. Rowling.

While the emphasis is on fact, not glorification, the books are meant to be fun to read. Each volume provides in-depth information about the subject's life from birth through childhood, the teen years and adulthood. A thorough account relates family background and education, traces

personal and professional influences, and explores struggles, accomplishments, and contributions. A timeline highlights the most significant life
events against a historical perspective. Bibliographies supplement the ref-
erence value of each volume.

PREFACE

In August 2001, Venezuelan President Hugo Chávez used the seventy-fifth birthday of Fidel Castro to describe Cuba's Maximum Leader as the Americas' "greatest revolutionary leader." Not all would agree with Chávez, but all would agree that Castro is among the most enduring, and that his impact upon the Americas is most profound.

Despite his career, scholarly analysis of Castro remains difficult because of his own reclusiveness and the scholar's inability to examine the decision-making progress within Cuba. Still, through the available literature and Castro's interviews, writings, and speeches, a picture emerges of a complex man. Early on, Castro came to understand the political corruption and skewed socioeconomic disparities within Cuba, and its economic dependence upon the United States. So too, did most Cubans, and Castro capitalized upon their demands for reform in order to lead a successful revolution that would result in a new Cuba. When he came to Havana in 1959, Castro did not bring plans on how to establish this new Cuba, only socialist ideas. Over the years, the path to a socialist Cuba confronted many obstacles, but Castro remained focused upon the ideal. In foreign affairs, Castro became a maverick who, for a brief moment, gained international prestige for Cuba. In essence, Fidel Castro is synonymous with the Cuban Revolution.

Castro also led a Revolution that vaulted him to political power; he maneuvered to become Cuba's Maximum Leader. Simply put, Castro became a political tyrant, eliminating political opponents, and suppressing dissent.

To be "great" as Chávez suggests, however, a leader must take into account the political and socioeconomic needs of the larger society he governs. While Castro may seek those ideals, he does not practice them. Just as any visitor to Cuba, Castro cannot escape the fact that Cuba is an enslaved society continuously enduring socioeconomic inequalities.

This volume is a narrative history of Castro and his Revolution, depicting its successes and its failures. In so doing, it verifies an often-used description of the four stages of revolution. First, a dictator or corrupt government is challenged through the established political means. For Castro, this was Cuba from 1947 to 1952. Second, the violent stage of revolution commences. In Cuba, this began when Fulgencio Batista silenced the legitimate means of protest with his 1952 coup d'état. It lasted from Castro's raid on the Moncada Army Barracks in 1953 until his march into Havana in January 1959. Third, the revolutionaries consolidate their power. This Castro accomplished by 1964 with the elimination, or silencing, of all opposition. Finally, the revolution is institutionalized. Castro legitimated his Revolution with the 1976 constitution and reaffirmed it with the implementation of his Rectification Program in 1986 and successive Communist Party Congresses in 1986, 1991, and 1997.

Castro's Revolution also illustrates the efficacy of the economic dependency theory. Although now widely discounted in favor of free markets and globalization, economic dependency asserts that a country's economic health is dependent upon a much stronger nation to which it is inextricably tied. No one doubts that from the mid-nineteenth century until the severance of diplomatic and economic relations in 1961, Cuba was dependent upon the United States. The latter was its major market for sugar and other goods and the primary supplier of consumer and manufactured goods. The relationship also created a financial dependency for Cuba. When the United States relationship ended, Castro cast about for another benefactor and, until its collapse in 1991, found one in the Soviet Union. With the Cuban economy on the verge of collapse in 2004, Castro continues to search for another benefactor, this time on his terms.

This volume includes a historical timeline of Fidel Castro's life and related significant events which will provide the reader with an overview of the book. This volume also includes a "Further Reading" section of the most salient works and a list of important documentaries about Castro and his Revolution. For those wishing to keep abreast of contemporary Cuba, significant Web sites are identified.

Words of appreciation go to Kevin Ohe and Steven Vetrano at Greenwood Press for making this opportunity possible and to the staff at Greenwood for seeing this project through to its completion. I am indebted to Bruce Latimer, head of the Documents Collection at the University of

North Florida, and a good friend, for assisting with the location of materials essential to this work. As always, to my wife, Yvonne, who continues to encourage and support all of us—our 6 children, their spouses, and our 14 grandchildren.

Thomas M. Leonard
Jacksonville, Florida
March 19, 2004

TIMELINE

1926   Fidel Castro is born on August 13 to Angel Castro and Lina Ruz González.

1927   University of Havana students establish the Directorio Estudiantil Universatario (DEU).

1933   President Franklin D. Roosevelt announces the "Good Neighbor Policy" by which he pledges the United States will not intervene in the internal affairs of Latin American Nations. Three years of political crisis end with the military ouster of President Gerardo Machado y Morales in August and the installation of Carlos Manual Céspedes. A month later, Fulgencio Batista leads the "Sergeants' Revolt" that overthrows Céspedes and replaces him with a provisional government headed by Ramón Grau San Martín.

1934   Batista overthrows President Grau in January and installs Carlos Mendieta as president. In May, the United States abrogates the Platt Amendment that granted it the right to intervene in Cuba's internal affairs.

1938   The Communist Party is granted legal status.

1940   A new constitution is promulgated, considered the most progressive in Latin America. Fulgencio Batista is elected president.

1941   Castro enrolls at Belén High School, where he excels in sports, but not as a student.

1944   The Communist Party changes its name to the Partido Socialista Popular (PSP). Ramón Grau San Martín is elected President of Cuba.

1945   Following graduation from Belén, Castro enrolls at the University of Havana to study law.

1947   Eduardo Chibás establishes the opposition Partido del Pueblo Cubano (*Ortodoxo*). Fidel Castro is the only university student member and gains public attention as critic of President Grau. Castro also escapes capture when his 1,200 would-be revolutionaries set out for the Dominican Republic where they intended to overthrow dictator Rafael Trujillo.

1948   Castro visits Bogotá, Colombia during the riots that resulted from the assassination of popular political leader Jorge Gaitán. Castro marries Mirta Díaz-Balart, daughter of a wealthy Cuban. In October, Carlos Prío Socarrás is elected President of Cuba.

1950   Castro graduates from Havana Law School and enters private practice, representing the poor against the Cuban government.

1952   Fulgencio Batista engineers a military coup to oust President Carlos Prío Socarrás. As a result, Castro concludes that the only way to change Cuba's corrupt political system is via a mass movement.

1953   Castro is sentenced to 15 years in prison for his leadership role in the unsuccessful attack upon the Moncada Army Barracks.

1955   After being freed from prison under a general amnesty, Castro leaves for Mexico to organize the 26th of July Movement as a force to return to Cuba with the intention of ousting Batista from office.

1956   December, Castro returns to Cuba aboard the yacht *Granma* to begin his guerrilla war against the Batista regime.

1957   *New York Times* reporter Herbert Matthews locates Fidel Castro and his guerrilla army in the Escambray Mountains, contradicting Fulgencio Batista's claim that the revolutionary group had been eliminated.

1958   The United States imposes an arms embargo upon the Batista regime. With his army in disarray and confronted with widespread civilian opposition, Batista flees to the Dominican Republic in the early hours of January 1, 1959.

1959   January 8, Castro arrives in Havana and within a month becomes Prime Minister. Immediately, he sets out to consolidate his power with summary trials and executions of *Batistianos* and enemies of the Revolution. During his visit to the United States in April, Castro asserts that he is not a communist. In May, the government enacts its sweeping Agrarian Reform Law.

1960   In February, Castro concludes a commercial treaty with the Soviet Union. In May, he nationalizes U.S.-owned oil refineries in Cuba. In July, President Dwight D. Eisenhower cuts the Cuban sugar quota. In response, Castro directs the nationalization of U.S. properties.

1961   In January, the United States severs diplomatic relations with Cuba. In March, the U.S. Congress imposes a trade embargo on Cuba. In April, the Central Intelligence Agency (CIA) sponsors the failed Bay of Pigs invasion. In December, Fidel Castro proclaims himself to be a Marxist-Leninist.

1962   At the United States's insistence, Cuba is expelled from the Organization of American States (OAS). In response, Castro issues the Second Declaration of Havana calling for revolutions across Latin America. Between October 22 and 28, the United States and the Soviet Union confront each other over the presence of Soviet missiles on the island. The crisis ends when the Soviets agree to remove their offensive weapons.

1963   Fidel Castro visits the Soviet Union for the first time.

1965   Castro establishes the new Partido Communista de Cuba (PCC). Ernesto "Che" Guevara is dismissed from government after his failed policies lead to a serious crisis.

1967   Guevara is killed in Bolivia. His death deals an irreversible blow to Castro's dream for spreading revolution throughout Latin America.

1968   The Cuban government inaugurates its "revolutionary offensive" with the nationalization of the remaining 65,000 private businesses and preparation for a 10-million-ton sugar crop in 1970.

1970   The sugar harvest totals only 8.5 million tons—short of the projected goal. The economy goes into a tailspin because of the government's overzealous efforts on sugar at the expense of other sectors. Castro admits personal responsibility for the failure and directs the restructuring of the Cuban economy with Soviet advice and assistance.

1975   The First Communist Party Congress convenes in Havana and elects Castro as its head. The Family Code is promulgated, establishing a comprehensive set of laws regulating

family, marriage, and divorce. Cuban troops enter the An-
golan Civil War against Portuguese colonial rule.

1976   A new socialist constitution is promulgated. The central government is reorganized around a Council of Ministers headed
by a president, Fidel Castro. In so doing, Castro also becomes
Head of State.

1977   Cuba and the United States establish "Interests Sections" in
each other's capitals.

1979   Fidel Castro is elected President of the Non-Aligned Movement during its sixth summit conference being held in Havana, but Castro's leadership is weakened later in the year
with the Soviet invasion of Afghanistan.

1980   Approximately 125,000 Cubans make their way to the
United States during the Mariel boatlift. Castro assumes per-
sonal control over the Ministries of Defense, Interior, Public
Health, and Culture.

1981   Jorge Más Canosa founds the Cuban American National
Foundation (CANF), which achieves significant influence
over U.S. policy on Cuba.

1983   Cuban military and construction workers are arrested as a result of the U.S. invasion of Grenada.

1985   The United States government inaugurates "Radio Martí" to
deliver allegedly unbiased newscasts into Cuba that, in reality, were anti-Castro. Cuba responds by suspending family
visits for Cuban Americans.

1986   Amidst pubic apathy and economic stagnation, Castro inaugurates a program of rectification in an effort to revive the
revolutionary spirit among the Cuban people. The Third
Party Congress reaffirms Castro's political power and the nation's commitment to socialism.

1989   Soviet Premier Mikhail Gorbachev visits Cuba and informs
Castro that trade relations between the two nations will soon
confront unspecified changes. Almost immediately, Castro
directs a public attack upon the Soviet system.

1990   The United States government inaugurates "TV Martí" to
send video propaganda into Cuba.

1991   The Soviet Union collapses and with it, all Soviet and East
European Bloc economic assistance ends. In response, Cuba's
Fourth Communist Party Congress adopts additional auster-
ity measures to mark the beginning of its "Special Period."
All Cuban troops are withdrawn from Angola.

1992   The United States enacts the Cuban Democracy Act, popu-
        larly known as the Torricelli Bill, which increases trade sanc-
        tions against Cuba, including the prohibition of trade
        between U.S. subsidiaries in third countries and Cuba. Presi-
        dent George H. W. Bush suspends its imposition, fearing re-
        taliation from the western world. Bill Clinton succeeded
        Bush, and he, too, suspended its imposition.

1993   The Cuban government legalizes dollar transactions and
        authorizes limited self-employment. The Russian brigade,
        sent to Cuba after the 1962 missile crisis, departs the
        island.

1994–95 Following another mass exodus of Cubans to Florida in the
        summer of 1994, the United States and Cuba reach a new ac-
        cord in May 1995 by which the United States will accept
        20,000 Cubans per year and the Cuban government will con-
        trol its illegal immigration. Castro visits China and Vietnam
        to study what free market reforms have been introduced there
        while retaining one-party political systems. The Cuban gov-
        ernment approves the opening of family restaurants and
        home-operated repair shops.

1995   The Cuban Air Force shoots down two Miami-based exile
        group planes, allegedly in international waters, which leads to
        passage of the U.S. Helms-Burton Bill that further tightens
        the U.S. embargo on Cuba. President Bill Clinton, like his
        predecessor George H. W. Bush, suspends the restrictions on
        U.S. subsidiaries operating in third countries on trading with
        Cuba.

1996   At the conclusion of the Fifth Communist Party Congress in
        October, there are no indications of Castro relinquishing po-
        litical power or changing policies. In November, the death of
        CANF president Jorge Más Canosa leaves a void in the lead-
        ership of the Cuban-American community.

1997   In January, Pope John Paul II becomes the first Catholic
        prelate to visit communist Cuba. In public speeches he criti-
        cizes Cuba's human rights record and calls upon the United
        States to lift its embargo.

2000   President George W. Bush announces that he will continue
        the U.S. embargo despite mounting domestic and interna-
        tional pressure to terminate it.

2002   In March, Castro cracks down on dissidents amidst growing
        food and other consumer shortages. In early May 2002, for-

mer President Jimmy Carter visits Cuba where he calls upon Castro to introduce democratic reforms and institute democratic government. Castro ignores the president's call, but in late May President Bush tightens restrictions on U.S. trade with, and travel to, Cuba.

Chapter 1

GROWING UP IN CUBA

Winds of change swept across Cuba during the 1920s. The landowning political elites—Liberals and Conservatives—that dominated the Cuban landscape since the island's independence in 1902 came under attack from newer
groups that demanded a place in the political arena, an end to government
corruption, tax and fiscal reform, improved trade relations with the United
States, and the termination of U.S. interference in the affairs of Cuba. A
new generation of entrepreneurs engaged in construction, real estate, production of consumer goods, and as managers of small sugar plantations all
formed associations to press their demands. University students also organized into the National Student Congress and demanded the removal of in-
competent faculty, student participation in university governance, and
increased government financial support for the universities. Working
women formed associations in the industries in which they labored—teachers, servants, launderers, dressmakers, seamstresses, and cigar workers. Their
Partido Nacional Sufragistas pressured for the enfranchisement of women.
The Confederación Nacional Obrera de Cuba (CNOC) brought together
an estimated 200,000 workers from 128 separate unions across Cuba. Along
with the Radical Socialist Party, the workers pressed for improved working
conditions, better wages, social benefits, and government regulation of key
industries. Nineteenth-century war veterans founded the National Association of Veterans and Patriots in 1923. Because its 12-point plan encom-
passed the demands of all groups, it captured the imagination of Cubans
across the social spectrum. At the time, President Alfredo Zayas y Alfonso
understood the national mood, but rather than address the issues, he silenced
the protest by banning public meetings and jailing or exiling opposition

leaders. Not so Gerardo Machado y Morales, a Liberal politician elected Cuba's president in 1924 on a "Platform of Regeneration."

The political machinations that dominated the city of Havana had little to do with the daily life in the small community of Birán, some 400 miles from Havana in northeastern Cuba, near the town of Mayari in Oriente Province (now Holguín Province). There, on August 13, 1926, on the family's sugar plantation, Fidel Castro was born, one of seven children, to Angel Castro and Lina Ruz González. Fidel's siblings included an older sister, Angela, an older brother, Ramón, a younger brother, Raúl, and three other sisters, Agustina, Emma, and Juanita. In addition, Fidel had a half-brother, Pedro Emilio, and a half-sister, Lidia. Angel Castro came to Cuba as a volunteer in the Spanish army during the War for Cuban Independence. When the war ended in 1898, he chose to stay on, seeking economic opportunities not available in his native Spain. Angel Castro cut sugar cane and worked as a day laborer before becoming a property owner and a successful sugar planter. Despite his wealth, Angel Castro remained frugal. The family home, Las Manacas, resembled an army barracks, not that of a successful sugar planter. Las Manacas stood on stilts, which Angel Castro expanded to meet the needs of his growing family, domestic servants, and farm laborers. The house was absent of musical instruments, works of art, and books. Despite Angel Castro's wealth, the family was not educated or socially mannered. The local elites of Birán and Mayari socially avoided the Castro family.

By the 1920s, the ambience of Oriente had changed. Most of the Cuban sugar planters had sold out to U.S. investors or been otherwise forced off their lands. They moved to Havana, where they built large homes. In their place stood U.S.-owned sugar plantations and mills. Angel Castro remained and prospered by selling his wood, cane, and cattle to the U.S.-owned businesses.

As a child, Fidel received little supervision or discipline from his parents. He wandered freely around the grounds, often shooting at animals with his father's guns and playing with the children of the farm workers, mostly Haitians and Afro-Cubans. Apparently, the accompanying poverty and racism escaped Fidel's young eyes. Not having been baptized, Fidel was labeled a Jew by his contemporaries. He developed a rebellious spirit, delivered expletive-ridden tirades, and exhibited a determination to have things his way. Although these traits made him a loner among his peers, Fidel Castro subsequently described his days at Las Manacas as the happiest days of his life.

Castro took these traits with him to Santiago de Cuba when his parents enrolled him at the La Salle School. At first, as a day student, Fidel lived with the local Haitian consul, who kept for himself a good portion of the stipend sent by Angel Castro to support his son. Nor did the consul encourage Fidel's academic career or expose the young Castro to the cosmopolitan life of Santiago. Fidel rebelled against these surroundings, causing Angel Castro to enroll his son as a boarder at La Salle. For a while, young Fidel took to learning and to his friendly companions, but he consistently refused to accept discipline from the Christian Brothers. Fidel soon lost interest in school. His indifference to education and contemptuous behavior caused Angel Castro to withdraw his son after the fourth grade.

Despite his dislike of school, Fidel wanted to return. His persistence caused Angel Castro to relent and for the fifth grade enrolled Fidel at Dolores Jesuit in Santiago, again as a day student, until he rebelled in the sixth grade. He again moved on campus but was unprepared for the challenge. Academically, Fidel fell behind. At first, he found a way to forge his grades and progress reports to his parents. Subsequently, Fidel took to rote memorization that contributed to his becoming a passable scholar. Socially, he remained apart from other students, most of whom came from elite families. To overcome their ridicule, Castro found acceptance, but not friendship, through athletics. Whatever his abilities, Fidel Castro came away from his early education impressed by the triumphs of the heroes of Cuban independence—Calixto García Iñiguez, Maximo Gómez y Báez, José Martí, and Antonio Maceo y Grajales—and U.S. President Franklin D. Roosevelt, whom Castro congratulated on his successful presidential re-election and from whom he requested "a twenty dollars bill american [sic]" in a 1940 letter. In each instance, Castro admired their leadership abilities more than anything else.

In September 1941 Fidel moved to Havana with his sister Angela, where he enrolled at the prestigious Jesuit administered Belén High School. Fidel owed his admission to a family friend, the Archbishop of Santiago, Enrique Pérez Serantes, not to his qualifying exams.

Before Castro moved to Havana, Cuba experienced dramatic changes. For two years following his election to the presidency in 1924, Gerardo Machado y Morales addressed the citizenry's varied protestations that emerged in the early 1920s. Machado pursued a policy of industrialization and economic diversification. As part of a massive public works program, the Cuban government began construction on the Central Highway to run the island's entire length. Agricultural credits provided for crop diversification and the 1927 Customs Law protected Cuba's fledgling industries. At the time, however, Cuba remained dependent upon the export of sugar and the price it brought in the world market. In 1928, world sugar prices dropped to 2.4 cents per pound and, with it, Cuba's government income dropped precipitously. A year later, the global depression struck, further damaging the Cuban economy. Over the next decade, the Cuban government participated in a number of schemes to revive the sugar industry.

As the economic crisis began, President Machado became increasingly repressive against the protesters from various socioeconomic groups. Through intimidation, coercion, and bribery, Machado was re-elected president of Cuba in 1928 which further intensified the opposition. The various groups formed earlier in the decade were now joined by more radical elements, such as the Directorio Estudiantil Universitario (DEU), the ABC Revolutionary Society and the newly-formed Partido Communista de Cuba (PCC). In the mid-1920s, the entry of thousands into the work force who could not find employment exacerbated the situation. Demonstrations and protests became violent. The Machado administration reacted with brutality and torture. Many of the opposition simply disappeared. By 1931, Cuba appeared to be in open warfare, but it had no visible impact upon the five-year-old Fidel Castro.

Amidst Cuba's disorder, U.S. President Franklin D. Roosevelt dispatched Assistant Secretary of State, Sumner Welles, as ambassador to Havana to mediate an end to the political conflict. Welles met with frustration as Machado stubbornly clung to the presidency, until his forced resignation on August 4, 1933. The situation continued to deteriorate under Provisional President Carlos Manuel de Céspedes y Quesada, until disgruntled university students found an ally in the noncommissioned officers, led by Sergeant Fulgencio Batista, who engineered a coup on September 4, 1933, that ultimately led to the provisional presidency of a socialist-minded university professor, Ramón Grau San Martín.

Until his ouster in January 1934, Grau introduced sweeping reforms that reflected the ideals of José Martí. The government decreed an eight-hour work day for Cuban workers, prohibited the importation of Haitian and Jamaican workers, and required that 50 percent of all employees in any company be Cuban. Grau proclaimed a land distribution program and ordered a reduction in interest rates to stimulate sugar production by small farmers. Significantly, women received the right to vote. Grau unilaterally abrogated the 1902 Platt Amendment that granted the United States the right to intervene in Cuba's internal affairs, but his action was nonbinding. The reform measures struck at Cuba's established sociopolitical order and the profits of U.S. companies operating across the island. At the same time, Cuba's Communist Party and National Confederation of Workers criticized Grau for not going further. Under pressure from both the left and the right, Grau sought the support of the old-line military officers, but they refused.

Despite the fact that U.S. policy had undergone significant change since the mid-1920s, resulting in Roosevelt's pronouncement of the Good Neighbor Policy in 1933, by which the United States pledged to no longer intervene in the internal affairs of Latin American nations, Ambassador Welles played a significant role in Grau's ouster in January 1934. Welles persuaded Roosevelt to withhold diplomatic recognition from Grau and, behind the scenes, he and his successor, Jefferson Caffrey, encouraged Batista to move against the Cuban president. Batista did. On January 15, Grau departed for Mexico City, to be replaced by Carlos Mendieta, whom the United States quickly recognized.

At the time, most Cubans understood the U.S. role in Grau's removal. While the old-line elite accepted this role, others outside this circle remained determined to implement political and social reform in Cuba. Many of the more moderate elements joined the *Auténtico* Party, founded in 1934 by a group of students who supported Grau's reform program and committed to reform through the electoral process. The more militant students and laborers formed *Jóven Cuba*, also in 1934. They turned to terrorism and violence against the Mendieta administration culminating in a general strike in March 1935. Batista used the army to break the strike, suppress the opposition student and labor leaders, and dismantle their organizations. The events of March 1935 clearly established Batista as the final arbiter of Cuban politics for the remainder of the decade. He ruled through puppet presidents: José A. Barnet (1935–36), Miguel Mariano Gómez (1936), and Federico Laredo Brú (1936–40).

Although these events ushered in a new era in Cuban politics by unleashing the demands of lower socioeconomic groups, they meant little to Fidel Castro, who, at the time, was an unhappy student in Santiago de Cuba.

Batista understood the winds of change and, in many ways, acted as a political populist. He directed the government to reach out to the urban disadvantaged via health programs, rent and utility rate controls, and consumer cooperatives. Batista also reached out to the rural poor with a modest agrarian reform program and the military's civic action programs in education, agriculture, hygiene, and nutrition. All working sectors benefited from the reorganization of Cuba's tax structure. Cuban nationalism was also satisfied in 1934 with the official abrogation of the Platt Amendment.

Batista also understood that the government operated under a cloud of illegality. To address the issue, a constitutional convention was convened in 1940. Cuba's 1940 constitution was considered one of the most progressive in the Western Hemisphere. It provided for a president, congress, and supreme court modeled after that in the United States and established a

national bank. The constitution recognized racial and sexual equality, provided for universal suffrage, free elections, and referenda, and sanctioned a
wide range of political and civil rights. The social provisions reflected the
goals of the Revolution of 1933: minimum wages and eight hour workdays,
worker's compensation, right to strike, and a proviso requiring that 50 percent of all jobs in a given firm be held by Cubans. In effect, the 1940 constitution brought to a close the revolutionary stirrings of the previous
decade, but because it lacked enforcement provisions, it also stood as an
agenda for future implementation by political leaders. That first leader
would be none other than Fulgencio Batista.

Amidst political turmoil dating to the late 1920s, the Cuban economy
became increasingly intertwined with that of the United States. As
Cuba's largest sugar market, U.S. policymakers were sensitive to the adverse impact that the global depression had upon the Cuban sugar industry. Beginning in 1934 with the Jones-Costigan Act and Reciprocal Trade
Treaty, the United States implemented a series of measures to ensure
Cuba a fixed share of the U.S. sugar market, rising from 25.4 percent in
1933 to 31.4 percent by 1940, and at a tariff 20 percent lower than that
levied on other foreign producers ($0.90 rather than $1.20 per pound). As
a result, during the 1930s, Cuban sugar production rose by 1 million tons
to 2.9 million tons and income nearly doubled to $120 million. The fig-
ures are deceiving because the U.S. measures did not end the sugar glut on
the world market. World War II did that, when European beet sugar and
Asian supplies were lost to the theaters of war.

The 1934 Reciprocal Trade Treaty granted the United States preferential rates on more than 400 agricultural and industrial items, whereas
Cuba received tariff preferences on 35 of its articles, mostly agricultural,
that amounted to 90 percent of Cuba's exports to the United States. In effect, Cuban manufacturing suffered a serious blow.

The U.S.-Cuban economic connection went far beyond trade. In the
two decades following Cuba's independence, the extent and diversity of
U.S. investments on the island multiplied. By the late 1920s, North
Americans dominated every economic sector: sugar, tobacco, railroads
and other transportation facilities, utilities, and tourism. The Great Depression of the 1930s did not alter the pattern.

Thus, as Batista commenced his presidency in 1940 and Fidel Castro
entered Belén High School in 1941, Cuba was in a state of flux. Implementation of the 1940 constitution rested on Batista's intentions, of
which the growing Cuban middle class remained unsure. The status of
Cuba's traditional elites and the security of U.S. investments on the island remained dependent upon the reliability of Batista and his army to

maintain order, and the wealth of the sugar and tobacco growers depended upon the availability and conditions of access to the U.S. market. Cuba's fledgling industrial class demanded protection against the ever-increasing presence of U.S. manufactured goods. Urban workers, particularly the estimated 300,000 who joined the newly formed communist-oriented Confederación de Trabajadores de Cuba (CTC), pressed their demands for improved salary and benefits, while protesting U.S. presence on the island. Despite their impoverished conditions, sugar and tobacco workers appeared on the periphery of the political spectrum, a source waiting to be tapped.

During his presidency (1940–44), Batista implemented many programs in public health, education, and social welfare. During World War II, his administration also benefited from the loss of sugar competitors in the European and Asian theaters, but the newfound wealth also heightened graft and corruption throughout government, a fact that cost him the support of the majority of Cubans. Batista worsened his image at home and with U.S. policymakers when he legalized the Cuban Communist Party, brought two of its members into his Cabinet as ministers without portfolio, and extended recognition to the Soviet Union. Still, he cooperated with the United States throughout the war, permitting the construction of defense sites and implementing an anti-Nazi program across the island. And to bolster his position at home, Batista visited with Roosevelt and Welles in Washington in December 1942. At the time, the U.S. administration did not want to interfere in Cuban politics, fearing that doing so might disrupt the nation and create an unwanted problem during World War II. The policy, however, did not prevent U.S. Ambassador Spruille Braden from criticizing the ineptitude and corruption of the Batista regime.

Batista did not challenge Ramón Grau San Martín's presidential electoral victory in 1944, nor his commitment to agricultural diversification and industrialization. The reality of world events changed that. World sugar production returned to its prewar levels by 1947, and with it Cuba's income drastically declined. Rather than turn to diversification, the Cuban sugar growers pressured Grau to obtain a larger share of the U.S. market. In addition, the leaders of Cuba's small industrial sector preferred tariff protection for their fledgling operations rather than open the country to foreign investment. At the same time, the CTC demanded the implementation of the 1940 constitution's labor provisions. The CTC also feared further U.S. investment on the island if Grau accepted the U.S. proposed Commercial Treaty that included funds for industrial diversification. Grau responded to Cuban nationalism, but further irritated the

United States by his refusal to extend wartime base agreements on the island. Thus, Grau left the presidency in 1948 as no friend of the United States and increasingly unpopular at home for having lost his zeal for the goals of the Revolution of 1933, for the corruption and nepotism that characterized his administration, and for the uncontrolled gangsterism that gripped Havana.

Castro was a witness to all this, first as a Belén High School student and subsequently while a student at the University of Havana. At Belén, Castro endured the same social ostracism that he experienced in Santiago. Belén was the most prestigious educational institution in Cuba at the time and attracted the sons of the elite families. Although Fidel later claimed that he easily made friends at the school, his classmates recalled otherwise. To them, Castro was crude, ill-mannered, and ill-tempered, and often was described as a "peasant." While Castro sought the recognition he gained at Birán and Santiago, the students at Belén came from the "best" families and, to them, Castro was a provincial who did not dress properly and acted silly with his foolhardy behavior. Although his excellence in sports—hiking, basketball, and baseball—earned him respect, Castro remained outside the school's inner social circles. Academically, Castro excelled only in those subjects that interested him—history, geography, and agriculture. He showed a keen interest in religious history, particularly battles like that at Jericho, and the heroic accomplishments of Moses, Joshua, and Prophet Daniel. At that time, most of the Jesuit instructors came from Spain, brought with them fascist ideas, and were strongly anticommunist. Furthermore, some of the priests predicted that war between the United States and Latin America was inevitable because of their disparate cultures. Yet, at the time Castro was a student, there is nothing to indicate that he was influenced by the Jesuit teachings, the corruption of the Batista regime, or the emergence of the communists as a potent political force in Cuban politics. Castro appeared apolitical. Twenty years later Castro cynically recalled his Jesuit education, describing it as rigid and stifling. Yet, even later, Castro explained that the Spanish Jesuits instilled in him a strong sense of dignity and a sense of justice. Castro's contradictory statements about his Jesuit education serve as a harbinger of his personal comments about revolutionary Cuba.

In September 1945, Fidel Castro moved on to the University of Havana's Law School confident that he would quickly influence his fellow students and gain notoriety as he had done at Dolores and Belén. But Castro faced new obstacles. Located near the center of Havana, students came to campus for class, to use the library, and to meet with professors. As a commuter institution, the university did not have dormitories, an organized sports program, or other amenities familiar to Castro. Without an organized sports program or a variety of social outlets, student life centered around café's where they discussed politics, their future careers, and ordinary matters. Castro took an apartment with his two sisters near the university. In addition to subsidizing the apartment, Angel Castro provided his children with a generous allowance and Fidel a new Ford automobile, which he used to impress people.

In sharp contrast to his previous structured and disciplined educational experiences, Castro entered a university where students wielded more power than administrators and poorly paid instructors were, for the most part, also poor teachers. Students could pass their exams without attending classes simply by memorizing the material. Cuba, like elsewhere in Latin America, went through sweeping educational reforms during the 1930s that resulted in autonomous universities free from government interference, including the intrusion of police or military forces. As a result of these reforms, the Federación Estudiantil Universitaria (FEU) wielded vast political power on campus. By the time of Castro's enrollment at the university, the FEU had become a vocal critic of government corruption. Students also formed a number of organizations, ostensibly to advocate social reforms, but in reality to gain their own influence through threats, intimidation, and terror. Many argue that by the time Castro began his law studies in 1945, the campus violence in Havana only mirrored that of the larger Cuban society.

If the uninformed and apolitical Fidel Castro was unprepared for the university's environment, save rote memorization for examinations, he quickly immersed himself in student politics and was soon recognized for his singular mind and independent action. Although elected a delegate to the FEU, Castro never advanced beyond that because he could not be a team player. Even the communist campus organization recognized that Castro would not succumb to its discipline. There were other outlets for someone seeking the limelight, particularly the Movimiento Socialisto Revolucionario (MSR) and the Unión Insùrrecional Revolucionaria (UIR). Led respectively by Rolando Masferrer and Emilio Tró, the MSR and UIR evolved into gangster groups, each committed to eliminating the other. Their offices were on the university campus, free from government or police interference. President Grau sought to control the groups by appointing members to the National Police. It didn't help. The violence continued. According to contemporary accounts, during his first year of law school, Castro joined the UIR after being rebuffed by the MSR, but that cannot be substantiated. He also joined the local Anti-Imperialist League and Free Puerto Rico student groups, both of which denounced

U.S. presence in the Spanish-speaking Caribbean islands since 1898. None of the groups could be identified as Marxist. Castro gained his first significant notoriety in Havana on November 27, 1946, the seventy-fifth anniversary of the execution of eight medical students by Spanish colonial authorities for their pro-independence activities. Speaking before the martyr's pantheon in the Colón cemetery, Castro used the occasion to denounce President Grau's political record and anticipated unconstitutional bid for re-election in 1948. His charge that Grau killed all hopes of the Cuban people earned Castro front-page coverage in the Havana newspapers the next day.

Castro did not return to Las Manacas when university classes ended for the holidays in December 1946, the first time since his student days at Santiago. He, instead, remained in Havana and, over the next year, became increasingly politically active. In so doing, Castro became committed to confrontation in order to achieve maximum public exposure. In January 1947 he helped draft and then signed, an FEU declaration against President Grau's re-election, pledging to work toward that end even it meant the signee's death. Next, he led a group of law students to the newly constructed prison on the Isle of Pines. Returning to Havana, Castro asserted that it was not the "model penitentiary" that Grau claimed, but a rat hole where prisoners lived in wretched conditions, received bad food, and were subjected to brutal treatment by the guards. On May 15, 1947, Castro, only two months shy of his twenty-first birthday and the only invited university student, joined forces with Senator Eduardo Chibás to break with the *Auténticos* and establish the Partido del Pueblo Cubano (PPC). It quickly became known as the *Ortodoxo* Party because of its claim to support the principles of José Martí. The *Ortodoxo* Party was the only political party Castro joined prior to the Cuban Revolution and, by all accounts, it was a marriage of convenience. Castro and Chibás disliked and distrusted each other, but each used the other for their own purposes. For Castro, the *Ortodoxos* provided a sense of legitimacy and provided another public forum as he campaigned on Chibás's behalf in the 1948 presidential election won by Carlos Prío Socarrás.

Meanwhile, at the university, Castro used the student newspaper to criticize campus violence and the institution's inadequate education. The high-water mark of his criticism came on July 16, 1947, at the inaugural session of the University of Havana's constituent assembly to create a modern administrative and educational charter for the institution. With emotional appeals and deft body language that still characterize Castro's public speeches, he used the occasion to indirectly criticize both President Batista and President Grau for their failed leadership and corruption, which spilled over into the gangs that terrorized and corrupted the university and the students' education. By this time, Castro appeared as the leading critic of all that was wrong with Cuba.

Castro's growing prominence caused both President Grau and the MSR leadership to determine that Castro had to abandon his ways. He was advised by Mario Salabarría, the top associate of MSR founder and chief of secret police, Rolando Masferrer, to stop his anti-gangster attitude or leave the university. Fearing for his life, Castro decided to temporarily leave Havana. He emerged again in July 1947 when the MSR organized, and the Education Minister, José Alemán, financed, a group of men to train for the overthrow of Dominican Republic dictator Rafael Trujillo. Castro viewed the plot as a noble cause and sought to join on. Only the intercession of a friend persuaded Masferrer to accept the Castro he personally distrusted. Castro joined the expeditionary force on the small, uninhabited cay of Confite off Cuba's northern coast. News of their son's latest adventure brought Angel and Lina Ruz Castro, along with his brother Ramón, to Confite to beg Fidel to withdraw from the mission. Their pleadings and Luz's tears failed to persuade Fidel. On September 15, 1947, Fidel Castro, with 1,200 colleagues, embarked for the Dominican Republic. The adventure ended almost immediately after it began. The U.S. government convinced the compliant President Grau that any invasion of the Dominican Republic would be disruptive to Caribbean security and raise questions about the viability of his own administration. On September 20, Grau ordered the Cuban navy to intercept the expedition in the Bay of Nipe and arrest its participants. At this point, Castro jumped ship to avoid capture, but what happened after that is open for speculation. According to Castro, he swam to shore through several miles of shark infested waters in full battle uniform, wearing his field boots and carrying his Thompson machine gun, and then walked several miles to the family home at Las Manacas.

When he returned to Havana, Castro was unprepared for final examinations, meaning he would need at least another year of study to complete his law degree. Although Castro continued to visit the cafés with his small following, for the remainder of 1947 he otherwise withdrew from political and social activities.

Castro did not remain in the background very long. In early January 1948, he was among the most visible mourners at the funeral of Communist labor leader, Jesús Menéndez, who had been shot by an army captain in Manzanillo. On February 12 that same year, Castro was among the students hospitalized as the result of a police beating during a student protest against a police violation of the university's autonomy the day before when they entered the university's grounds. In September 1948, Castro joined his fellow students in demonstrating against President Grau's approval of an increase in bus fares.

During 1948, Castro was twice linked to politically motivated assassinations. Although the charges could not be proven, Castro used the incidents to advance his own cause. Following the February 22 assassination of Manolo Castro, the founder of the MSR, Fidel Castro and four other students were arrested and detained. He was considered the most likely suspect responsible for the shooting. Due to a lack of evidence, Castro was released the next day. He immediately held a news conference at the police station. Castro accused Masferrer of wanting him out of the way so that he, Masferrer, could take over control of the university. Then, on June 6, university policeman Oscar Fernández was shot in front of his own home. Before dying he and other witnesses identified Castro as the assailant. Claiming that this was a ploy by police agents that would result in his own assassination, Castro publicly asserted that he would never appear before a judge. The incident passed.

Castro gained greater notoriety as a result of the assassination of Colombian Liberal Party and labor leader, Jorge Eliécar Gaitán, on April 9, 1948. At the time, the Argentinian government of Juan Perón sent agents to Havana to recruit Cubans for anti-American demonstrations during the Inter-American Conference scheduled for Bogotá. Castro and fellow student Rafael del Pino expressed interest in going and the Argentine embassy in Havana financed their trip. The two went to enjoy themselves, not so much to join in the anti-U.S. demonstrations. That changed following Gaitán's assassination. Bogotá's streets became a scene of mob violence and property destruction brought about by the frustrated Liberals and the poor who idolized Gaitán. In addition, university students occupied government buildings and the national radio station and called for a general strike. Castro and del Pino left their room at the Claridge Hotel to join the mobs, but they were easily identifiable because of their white linen suits which contrasted to the tropical clothing worn by the Colombians. Castro also visited the national university campus, but found the students there unprepared to openly challenge governmental authority. Although U.S. Secretary of State, George C. Marshall concurred with the Colombian press that international communists instigated the riots, Colombia's Conservative Party government blamed foreigners in general, including the two Cubans in the white linen suits, erroneously identified as Walter Castro and Rafael D'Acquino. The two Cuban students found refuge in the Argentine Embassy until April 13, when they returned to Havana on a Cuban plane, rescued by the government they each despised. At a Havana press conference, Castro described the Colombian charges as libelous and asserted that neither he nor del Pino had contacts with any party in Colombia, including the communists. Subsequently, Castro claimed that the *Bogotázo* (riots in Bogotá) significantly influenced his understanding of the need to educate the Cuban people toward a revolution and to avoid anarchy, violence, and looting following the success of its revolution. Whatever lessons Castro learned from the *Bogotázo*, at the moment he increased his visibility among the Cuban people.

Cuba's 1948 presidential election only reinforced Castro's lesson from Bogotá regarding the need for a mass movement to change the course of Cuban politics. In the days leading up to the June 1 elections, Castro campaigned, particularly in his home province of Oriente, on behalf of the *Ortodoxo* Party candidate, Eduardo Chibás, who ran on a platform promising government honesty. Castro described the election as a battle between ideals and vested interests, Chibás representing the former, and Carlos Prío Socarrás, the latter. Castro also used the campaign to distinguish himself from Chibás when discussing the need for social reform. The opposition's efforts were to no avail. The Grau administration undertook a public works program and a huge public relations campaign to shore up the image of its official candidate, Carlos Prío Socarrás. In addition, the *Auténticos* spent an estimated $6 million, most of it government funds, on behalf of Prío. To ensure his victory, the government also intimidated voters and resorted to election day fraud. Prío won the June 1 election with 46 percent of the vote. Chibás came in a distant third with 16 percent behind the Liberal–Democratic coalition candidate Ricardo Nuñez. The Communist Party, which Castro had avoided since becoming a political activist, received 8 percent of the vote. In the immediate post-election period, Castro enhanced his reformer's image by driving throughout Havana clamoring against the electoral fraud.

On the day of Prío's inauguration, October 10, 1948, Castro was in Oriente preparing for his marriage to Mirta Díaz-Balart at her family home in Banes, not far from the Castro residence at Birán. The two met at the University of Havana, where Mirta was a philosophy student. The Díaz-Balarts were a wealthy and well-connected family, including links to Fulgencio Batista, who gave the newlywed Castros a $1,000 cash wedding gift. In contrast, Castro's family did not share the social and political prominence of the Díaz-Balart's, and Fidel, with his image as a university "gangster," was at odds with Cuba's established order. Following their marriage, the young Castros enjoyed a lengthy honeymoon in the United States at the expense of Angel Castro. Although Fidel considered enrolling at Columbia University, he returned to Havana to complete his law studies, again with his father's support.

Castro graduated from the University of Havana in September 1950, without achieving the distinction that he experienced at the Dolores or Belén schools. Despite his efforts, Castro did not hold significant elective offices in the university's student government and for the most part stood aloof from organizations and groups that required a commitment. Castro trusted few of his student colleagues, which contributed to his preference for acting independently. Although Castro had some followers and was often at the forefront of student protests, his gangster image did little to attract a supportive campus audience. Castro's attacks upon government corruption and calls for programs to support the poor were generally viewed as a means to attract attention, rather than a statement about his political and social philosophy.

Following graduation, Castro opened a Havana law office with fellow graduates Jorge Aspiazo Nuñez de Villavicencio and Rafael Resende Viges. The practice, which focused upon the causes of the poor and underrepresented people of Havana, was not successful during the three years of its existence. In fact, the firm won only two court decisions worth $4,800 combined. Castro lost interest in the profession, preferring to spend his time speaking out against government graft and corruption and the needs of the poor. For example, in November 1950 he was arrested for a student-led antigovernment demonstration in the city of Cienfuegos and he used his trial to issue a stinging criticism of the Prío administration for denying civil rights to the Cuban people. On another occasion he published an essay in the Havana newspaper *Alerta* in defense of Cuban laborers and peasants being exploited by industrialists and landowners. Castro also enrolled in some courses at the University of Havana in order to use student publications to attack government graft and corruption. On international issues he took a strong anti-United States stance. In 1950, Castro spoke out against the U.S. involvement in the Korean War and a year later stirred public opinion sufficiently to stop President Prío from sending troops to Korea on the United Nations side. Castro also called for Puerto Rico's independence from the northern tyrants.

Attracted to politics, Castro again sought to attach himself to the *Ortodoxo* Party leader, Eduardo Chibás. But the popular politician remained distant from Castro, whom Chibás considered abrasive and uncultured. Chibás contended that Castro's gangster reputation would only harm the *Ortodoxos* reform image. Castro, however, remained persistent. In an effort to gain acceptance, Castro constantly visited the party office headquarters in Havana. He visited Havana's poorest districts, delivered hundreds of speeches and radio addresses, wrote numerous editorials for *Alerta*, and distributed thousands of handbills and broadsides. Castro consistently emphasized government corruption and Cuba's need for responsible leadership. Although he addressed the needs of the poverty stricken, no clear social ideology emerged. In addition to being disliked and mistrusted by reformist politicians, the notoriety that Castro earned from his machinations also contributed to his heightened dislike by government officials.

Castro's varied activities not only kept him from the failing law practice, but also from his family. His wife, Mirta, often complained about Castro's constant absence, his inattention to their son, Fidelito, and his lack of responsibility to provide basic needs for the family. More than once, Mirta had to rely on family and friends for money to pay the rent, buy food, and meet installment payments on furniture. Life with Fidel was a far cry from that she knew growing up in the Díaz-Balart family. Outwardly, at least, Castro seemed indifferent to these matters.

As the 1952 presidential election approached, Cuba appeared in disarray and provided Castro yet another opportunity to gain notoriety. Added to this, the corruption and graft of Prío's administration placed the *Auténticos* in a vulnerable position. The opportunity seemed ripe for *Ortodoxo* Eduardo Chibás. Of the other political parties, only the Communist Party, reorganized as the Partido Socialista Popular (PSP) in 1944, was considered a significant player. In the Cold War atmosphere of the time, however, the Prío administration restricted its activities, confiscated its radio station, and harassed the party newspaper, factors that actually contributed to the party's popularity.

The political landscape changed appreciably on Sunday evening, August 5, 1951, when Chibás shot himself at the close of his weekly radio show. His popularity could be measured by the number of people who visited his casket in the Hall of Honor at the University of Havana and the size of the subsequent cortege to Colón cemetery. His death meant that the *Ortodoxos* lost their standard bearer. It also opened the door to intense political maneuvering.

Subsequently, the *Auténticos* selected Carlos Hevía, a graduate of the U.S. Naval Academy and an engineer with a reputation of honesty, as their presidential candidate. The *Ortodoxos* chose University of Havana Professor Roberto Agramonte as their presidential candidate. The political waters became more muddied when Fulgencio Batista, former strongman and president (1940–44), returned from Florida to seek the presidency as the candidate of the newly formed Unitary Action Party. But each of these parties needed the support of the minor parties—Nationalist, Liberal,

Democratic, Popular Socialist, and Republican—to win the election. The maneuvering for their support intensified in early 1952 and in February, all but the Popular Socialists announced their support for the *Auténtico* candidate, Carlos Hevía. The *Ortodoxo* candidate, Roberto Agramonte, refused the PSP's offer of support as he ran on an anticommunist platform.

As the campaign advanced, incumbent President Prío used the power and finances of the national government on behalf of Hevía. The support enabled him to buy more radio airtime, print more broadsides and handbills, and to travel throughout the island where large rallies were orchestrated on his behalf. The political opposition and the popular press attacked this misuse of government funds. Popular polls indicated the general public's disgust with the campaign's direction. The polls also indicated that Agramonte was the most popular candidate and that Batista had no chance of winning the election.

Recognizing the inevitable, Batista decided to seize the presidency. He turned to a group of junior army officers who had grown tired of the same things that motivated their predecessors in 1933—poor pay, lack of opportunities for promotion, and the supplemental perks available to senior officers. Coming largely from Cuba's middle class, they shared the populace's frustration with the corruption of Prío's regime and his coddling of the gangsters that roamed Havana's streets. These junior officers began to plot in the summer of 1951 and, in need of a person with national prominence, sought out Batista. He rejected the initial offer, believing that he could regain the presidency through the ballot box. When he realized otherwise in late February and early March 1952, Batista accepted the offer. In the early hours of Sunday, March 10, the officers acted. Senior officers were arrested and taken, without resistance, to Batista's estate outside Havana. Other rebel officers seized the radio and television stations. President Prío attempted to rally the troops, but could find none to support his cause, and the national congress refused his call to convene. Recognizing the inevitable, Prío gained asylum in the Mexican embassy and on March 13 was granted asylum in Mexico.

The coup was complete. When Havana returned to work on Monday, March 11, all appeared normal. Shops and businesses opened, vendors sold lottery tickets and newspapers, and the police directed traffic. There were no riots. Only the CTC labor leaders called for action. Fearing that Batista would return labor leadership to the communists, the CTC leadership called for a general strike, but it failed to materialize. The U.S. embassy in Havana reported to the State Department that, although concerned with Batista's unannounced intentions, most Cubans appeared satisfied with the ouster of the corrupt Prío administration.

Until the coup, Castro remained active in Havana politics, seeking publicity on every occasion. Most likely because of his connections to the Díaz-Balart family, Castro met with Batista shortly after he returned to Cuba in 1950. Although no record exists of their conversation at Batista's palatial Kukuine estate outside of Havana, one can only conclude that they used the meeting to determine the other's intentions, but, clearly, they were not allied. At the time of Chibás's death in August 1951, Castro stood vigil for 24 hours at his casket in the Hall of Honor at the University of Havana and a picture of him doing so appeared in most of Havana's newspapers and magazines. He also delivered a statement to the five radio stations covering the funeral, but failed to convince the *Ortodoxo* Party leadership to march Chibás's body before the national palace. Castro gained extensive publicity during the fall of 1951 when he organized mass rallies and demonstrations against the government for its plans to evict, and then tear down, the slum housing in Havana's La Pelusa district (today's Revolutionary Square) without compensating the slum dwellers. The Public Works Ministry succumbed to the pressure and promised to pay 57 pesos for each residence in the area, but Batista reneged on the promise after coming to power in March 1952. Castro continued his speeches to the residents of Havana's poorer districts, distributed broadsides and flysheets throughout the city, and increased his radio talk time. He pursued a common theme: the government had a responsibility to improve the quality of life for the poor people.

Castro also continued Chibás's investigation into government corruption. On January 28 and February 19, 1952, Castro issued several charges against Prío. Most sensational was the presidential pardon of wealthy businessman and Prío friend, Emilio Fernández Mendigutía, who had been convicted of raping a nine-year-old girl. Castro also revealed that Prío increased his personal landholdings by elevenfold to 1,994 acres since 1948 and turned these properties into luxurious estates. Castro also reported that Prío used prison and military labor to cultivate the crops on these estates for his private profit. Added to this were the usual charges of government graft, approval of police and military brutality, catering to Havana's gangster crowd, and the assignment of inflated government contracts to friends.

Although Castro's vehemence may have earned him an audience among the poor, it did not endear him to the leading political actors. In February 1952, at the time of Castro's second set of charges against the Prío administration, Castro's friends feared for his life. Despite his constant presence at the *Ortodoxo* Party headquarters, the party leadership did not share Castro's belief that he should pick up Chibás's mantle. In fact, the party leadership distanced themselves from Castro's firebrand tactics. On the eve of Batista's March 10 coup d'état, the *Ortodoxo* Party had not endorsed his candidacy for the national House of Representatives. Because of his independent attitude and action, Castro refused to accept the discipline required to join the communist PSP. Nor did his political rhetoric, which focused upon government corruption and misdeeds, indicate his sharing of the party's socialist agenda. In typical Castro fashion, he contradicted himself about the events of 1952. Thirteen years later, in 1965, he told a U.S. visitor that he was neither a Marxist nor a communist at that time, a statement he contradicted in 1983.

Whatever Castro's political thinking at the time, Batista's March 1952 coup d'état blocked Castro's road to national political prominence unless he chose to capitalize on his connection with the Díaz-Balart family to seek a position within the new Batista administration. He did not. Instead, Castro chose his own course of action.

In the days immediately following the coup d'état, Castro attacked Batista for his usurpation of power. On Sunday, March 16, 1952, he joined with other *Ortodoxos* at the Colón cemetery to commemorate the anniversary of Eduardo Chibás's death. Castro used the occasion to publicly challenge the Cuban people to oust Batista by force. A week later, Castro filed a brief in a Havana court charging Batista with violating the constitution by implementing the coup and asserting that he should be sentenced to 100 years in prison. On April 6, Castro again challenged the Cuban people to rebel against the regime as the only way possible to correct the situation. By issuing these attacks, Castro was convinced that the government wanted to arrest him. This fear prompted Castro to move nightly about Havana in clandestine fashion. But he was never arrested, either because of family connections or because the *Batistianos* did not consider him an important opposition figure. During this time period, Castro concluded that neither the university students nor traditional political parties would do more than issue letters of protest, conduct an occasional demonstration, and sit around Havana's cafés lamenting Cuba's fate. They were no longer effective tools for change. Batista made special efforts to harass the communist's PSP, its labor leaders and its daily newspaper, *Hoy*. These measures pleased the United States and at the same time validated Castro's conclusion that the communists were politically weak and malleable.

After the Batista regime restored civil liberties on May 19, 1952, opposition to the regime became more prevalent. In response, the government suppressed individuals and groups that advocated change. Among the more important groups was that formed by Rafael García Bárcena, a professor at the Superior War College. In July 1952, its plot to overthrow Batista was uncovered and 40 of its members were arrested, only to be re-leased 2 days later with warnings to terminate their activities. They did not and, in fact, invited Castro to join their ranks. He refused, describing their plan to attack Camp Columbia as suicidal and disappointed at not being offered a leadership role.

More significant was a group of four people Castro encountered by chance at the Colón cemetery on May 1, where they had gathered to lay a wreath at the grave of labor leader Carlos Rodríguez, who had been killed by two policemen that Castro took to court on murder charges. The group included Abel Santamaría and Jesús Montané, respectively an accountant and human resource officer for General Motors, Melba Hernández, a lawyer and Haydée Santamaría, sister of Abel. Subsequently, they met regularly at the Santamaría apartment to discuss the works and writings of Eduardo Chibás and José Martí. The group also published a mimeographed anti-Batista bulletin, Son Los Mismos. Intrigued, Castro joined the group and soon appeared as its indisputable leader. Over the next several months new recruits were added, but in cell-like fashion, so that only Castro and the original four knew all the members. The group's initial emphasis was to attack the Batista regime through the newly named bulletin, El Acusador. Under the alias Alejandro, his middle name, Castro contributed stinging editorials about the Batista regime. He also continued to contribute to the university communist publication, Mella.

In September 1952, Castro went beyond public propaganda. At his instruction, military training exercises began; but the acquisition of arms was another matter. Without funds, black market matériel was unavailable. Castro drove to Birán to ask his father for $3,000. Unimpressed, Angel donated only $140 and advised his son to pursue a more promising career. Others were more generous, the most benevolent being Mario Muñoz, a medical doctor in Oriente Province, who donated $10,000 and two shortwave transmitters.

At the time, Castro's group was only one of many that opposed Batista. Some estimate there were as many as 100 opposition groups. Whatever the number, most were middle class in origin, bringing together teachers, students, professionals, small shopkeepers, and the like. Among the most notable organizations were the Movimiento Nacional Revolucionaria (MNR), founded by Rafael García Bárcena's, a professor at the University of Havana and the Superior War College, and the Acción Libertadora (AL) founded by politician Dr. Justo Carrillo. Owing to his mistrust of the middle class and determination to lead his own movement, Castro rejected any linkage to these groups.

Castro's group caused the government enough concern to prompt authorities to move against it on August 16, 1952, the first anniversary of Eduardo Chibás's death. That day, Castro's supporters intended to distribute copies of El Acusador charging Batista with the most venal sins and promising a revolution. The police intervened. The secret police also discovered the location of the mimeograph machine and one of the two shortwave radio transmitters. Each was destroyed. In all, four Castro supporters were arrested: Abel Santamaría, Melba Hernández, Joaquín González, and Elda Pérez. The two women were released the following day. Castro, in his capacity as a lawyer, pleaded for the release of the other two. Although his group appeared broken, Castro remained determined to topple Batista through violence.

Castro's increased political activities took a further toll on his marriage. Mirta became increasingly reliant upon support and handouts from family and friends. Castro's constant absence, including during a brief hospitalization of their son, Fidelito, strained the relationship to the limits. It was tested again in November 1952, when, by chance, Fidel was introduced to Naty Revuelta, and their relationship soon evolved into an affair.

From his boyhood days at Las Manacas through his political activism in 1952, Fidel Castro developed an independent mind and a determination to gain recognition and respect from the various publics he encountered, even if it meant using confrontational and violent means. Clearly, he wanted to work on his own.

Chapter 2

FROM MONCADA TO HAVANA

In the year following Batista's March 10, 1952, coup d'état, Cuba and, particularly, Havana presented the world with a new ambience. In place of the gangsterism and violence that characterized the capital city during late 1940s, *House Beautiful,* in its December 1952 issue, found Havana aglow with glittering night shows, sidewalk cafés with all-girl bands, and the excitement of jai alai matches, horse racing, and gambling run by the U.S. Mafia, at the city's must luxurious hotels. During the same time period, the Batista administration inspired confidence in the business circles. That confidence was expressed in significant private investment, which diversified the country's agriculture (especially into rice and cattle) and led to the establishment of a number of new industries (petroleum refining, mining, and miscellaneous manufacturing).

But all was not well in Cuba. The glitter and economic progress did not reach all of Cuba's social sectors. Batista continued to have opposition leaders arbitrarily arrested and detained and otherwise harassed. Batista also suppressed or co-opted labor union leaders. As the year passed, government brutality and corruption became more wide spread. The government's lavish public works program failed to absorb the chronic and large-scale number of unemployed workers, estimated at 8 percent and reaching to 20 percent during the 8–9 month dead season, during which sugar cane workers sat idle. At the same time the country's export earnings and available credit were not sufficient to meet the demands of the development program. The greatest problem that Cuba faced was a significant increase in its population and dependence on sugar. The U.S. Commerce Department and Cuban National Bank understood this and

the concomitant challenge of trying to improve living standards of Cuban
people.

Until August 1952, Castro and his followers appeared content to attack the wrongs of the Batista regime through the press, mimeographed
circulars, and public protest. Batista's crackdown on Castro and his followers on August 16 further convinced Castro that violence was the only
route to Batista's ouster. Batista's continued suppression of political opponents also forced Castro to become more secretive in his actions. Increasingly, he trusted fewer and fewer people. Castro's new attitude became
apparent in late August 1952, when he and Abel Santamaría drove
around the island to recruit an armed force. The recruits were organized
into cells of 10 in their hometowns and did not know their counterparts
in other cells. The recruits came from all walks of Cuban life—wealthy
families to those who worked for hourly wages. For example, one cell included a medical doctor, lawyer, musician, auto mechanic, watchmaker,
taxi diver, chauffeur, two cooks, and a parking lot attendant. None were
known communists and all were drawn together only by their dislike of
the Batista regime. By the end of 1952 Castro claimed to have 200 such
recruits.

Castro was not alone in the desire to oust Batista by force. The regime's
continued repression of civil society and the ever-worsening economic
conditions for the Cuban worker prompted the crystallization of other opposition groups. The Asociación de Amigos de Arelliano (AAA), sponsored by the Auténtico Party, imported arms and supported the training of
armed units. Another important opposition group, although not yet committed to insurrection, was the AL, founded by the former head of Cuba's
Agricultural and Industrial Development Bank Dr. Justo Carrillo. Carrillo
hoped to engineer a bloodless coup in cooperation with dissident officers
at Camp Columbia on April 5, 1953. It failed miserably. The most visible
was Rafael García Bárcena's MNR. Bárcena, who taught at the University
of Havana and the Superior War College and was a well-respected community leader, led a failed attack upon Camp Colombia in July 1952. Representatives of the opposition groups, save Castro and the communists
(neither of which were invited), gathered in Montreal, Canada in June
1953, but they failed to agree upon a common strategy to oust Batista from
office. Instead, the meeting verified the inability of the Auténticos and
Ortodoxos to lead the Cuban opposition against Batista.

The emergence of groups committed to the violent overthrow of
Batista forced Castro to think that his organization might lose its initiative and he his place in history. He determined to accelerate his plan of
action. By mid-February 1953, Castro and Abel Santamaría commenced

plans for an attack on the Moncada Army Barracks in Santiago de Cuba, combined with a simultaneous attack upon the army barracks at Bayamo, 80 miles to the west, in order to prevent reinforcements from reaching Santiago. The arms and munitions at each barracks would be distributed to their growing number of followers and the surrounding mountain ranges would provide the revolutionaries with safe haven from the national army. Ultimately, the two dreamed that their movement would become a nationwide effort to oust the Batista regime.

Castro and his closest advisors targeted Moncada because of its distance from Havana and set the attack date for July 26, a carnival time in Santiago that would help provide cover for the assault. In April 1953, Castro enlisted Ernesto Tizol Aguilera, a Sears Roebuck employee, to rent a two-acre farm in Siboney, some 15 miles from Santiago, ostensibly to pursue his part-time endeavor as a poultry farmer. Over the next few months Castro shipped to the farm arms and munitions to be used for the assault upon the Moncada and Bayamo Army Barracks. Often the arms arrived in packages labeled as "chicken feed." On the same road as the farm was the home of Moncada's commander, Colonel Alberto del Río Chaviano. Despite his passing in front of the farm every day, Chaviano never received a hint of the forthcoming attack. Another longtime Castro operative, Melba Hernández, persuaded an army officer, who subsequently joined the group, to obtain more than 100 army uniforms to which she and Haydée Santamaría stitched insignias. Santiago resident and fellow conspirator Renato Giotart obtained a copy of Moncada's floor plan. Eventually, Castro identified 150 men from the various cells around the country to lead the assault. Others would subsequently join in, including Castro's brother Raúl, who returned to Cuba in early July from a several month visit to Eastern Europe that included participation in the Soviet sponsored World Youth Congress in Vienna. Castro viewed the attack as the beginning of a larger war against Batista. Win or lose, and unless Fidel lost his life, he expected to retreat into the Sierra Maestra.

During the third week of July 1953, Castro's revolutionaries, traveling singularly or in pairs, made their way to Siboney by bus, car, and train. Before leaving Havana, Castro visited with his brother-in-law and Deputy Secretary of Interior, Rafael Díaz-Balart ostensibly to check upon the status of one of his jailed supporters. The real purpose, however, was to determine if government authorities suspected the attack on Moncada. Castro left the meeting convinced that he was free to act, a conviction that further bolstered his confidence in the success of the mission. In reality, the attack upon Moncada appeared suicidal. Castro counted upon the element of surprise by his approximately 200 poorly trained

and equipped men to overcome Moncada's thousand man garrison, with
greater firepower.

Castro's supporters arrived in Santiago at designated hotels and board-
ing houses not knowing their mission. Only Castro and four others knew
the objective. On the evening of July 25, the would-be army made its way
to the farm house in Siboney. There, they received the ill-fitting army
uniforms and assorted rifles, ranging from hunting and .22 caliber rifles to
an ancient machine gun and revolvers to be used in the attack. Even Castro's uniform did not fit properly. Each was given a black belt to distinguish themselves from Batista's soldiers. Castro laid out the three-pronged
assault plan. The first unit was to seize the all-important Post 3 that secured Moncada's main entry gate and courtyard. Once taken, the following forces would take control of the surrounding dormitories and their
occupants and then take control of the radio station and fan out among
the barracks with the newly captured weapons. A second unit would seize
the hospital and then fire upon the rear of the barracks. The third unit was
to take the Palace of Justice and from its rooftop neutralize the machine
guns on top of the barracks inside the fort. Dr. Mario Muñoz, Melba
Hernández, and Haydée Santamaría followed to provide any necessary
medical assistance to their fallen comrades.

At 3 A.M. Castro delivered to his troops, the "Moncada Manifesto,"
which he planned to read over the radio once the barracks were secure.
The "Manifesto" reflected Castro's fascination with Cuba's historic past
and its heroes, rather than an expression of a definitive political ideology.
The revolution, Castro asserted, drew upon the ideals of José Martí, Antonio Guiteras, Eduardo Chibás, and Cuba's 1940 constitution. He spoke
about implementing a meaningful democracy with civil and social justice,
not an autocratic state, nor a state-directed economy and privileges for
only a few. Although Castro did not expect the soldiers at Moncada to
offer stiff resistance in support of Batista, he warned that some of his followers might not survive the attack, but all could rejoice in that they were
fighting for the freedom of the fatherland. Not all were persuaded by Castro's exhortation. At 5 A.M., as the cars departed from the farm for the
Moncada Army Barracks, 10 men remained behind, with instructions not
to depart from the farm until after the raid was completed. They did not
wait that long. The exact number of men who took part in the raid remains unknown. Estimates range from 87 to 165.

The assault failed shortly after it began. As planned, the soldiers
opened Moncada's main gate to the uniformed rebels, but they quickly
recognized their mistake and the situation rapidly deteriorated for the
rebel forces. More troops were in the barracks than had been anticipated,

brought there to enjoy the carnival season. Nor did Renato Giotart's surveillance of the fort take into account the so-called "Cossack Patrol," a group of roving jeep patrols around the fort brought in for the carnival period. The radio station and other facilities had been moved since Giotart obtained the stronghold's floor plan. Although 50 rebels entered Moncada's courtyard, they quickly suffered heavy causalities before being driven out. The expected reinforcement never arrived. Castro's 10 hesitant soldiers left the farm at Siboney earlier than directed and drove into Santiago. None of the drivers knew the city streets and when the lead car turned away from the convoy an unknown number of other cars followed.

Fidel's other units were temporarily more fortunate. Lester Rodríguez and Raúl Castro led a successful attack upon the Palace of Justice and for a while provided protective cover to those in the courtyard. Abel Santamaría's 20-man force, accompanied by Dr. Muñoz, Melba Hernández, and Haydée Santamaría, momentarily took over the Santurnino Lora Hospital. As Castro's forces retreated from Moncada's courtyard, the others recognized the futility of their positions. Rodríguez and Raúl Castro abandoned the Palace of Justice. With the assistance of the hospital staff, the Santamarías, Muñoz, and Hernández dressed in hospital garb and took refuge in empty beds until uncovered by the intrusive army troops. In all, the battle lasted a little more than an hour. The army counted 13 *Fidelistas* dead and another 20 wounded. Among the dead was Dr. Muñoz who was shot in the head at point blank range after surrendering. About 40 *Fidelistas* made it back to Siboney; an unknown number of others made their way back to Havana. Rodríguez, a native of Santiago, lay down his gun and walked home. Raúl Castro also walked away, sleeping in sugar cane fields at night, before he was captured by an army patrol. Fidel Castro and 18 others escaped to the Sierra Maestra until August 1 when a regular army patrol stumbled upon them. Fortunately for Fidel, the patrol's commander, Lieutenant Pedro Manuel Sarría, was a friend from their days together at the University of Havana. He delivered Castro and his men to the civilian police in Santiago rather than the military authorities. The publicity surrounding Fidel's arrival in Santiago most likely spared him the torture, if not death, endured by other *Fidelistas* at the hands of the *Batistianos*.

Fidel's would-be revolutionaries met a similar fate at Bayamo. A week prior to the assault, 27 men assembled at a motel rented for that purpose. On the eve of the attack Fidel Castro met with the men and delivered the same inspirational message that he did at Siboney. Led by Raúl Martínez Arará, the entourage, wearing the ill-fitting army uniforms and carrying inadequate arms, marched upon the barracks at Bayamo in the early morning hours of July 26. When they reached the barracks' gates, one of the *Fidelistas* fired upon the horse tender, setting off a stampede and awakening the troops inside. The 2 groups exchanged gunfire for 15 minutes. Arará claimed that he lost only two men; the remainder were either captured or disappeared into the countryside.

In all, some 80 men from both sites were taken prisoner by the Batista army. Before being taken from Santiago to the provincial prison at Boniato to await trial, the men endured brutal torture, and even death, at the hands of their captors. For example, Abel Santamaría had his eyes gouged and presented to his sister Haydeé. In contrast, Fidel's two female followers, Haydeé Santamaría and Melba Hernández, were not physically harmed during their detention.

Batista immediately blamed the Moncada attack upon the traditional politicians who opposed him, such as Emilio Ochoa, José Pardo Llada, Carlos Prío Socarrás, and the communists. Batista also immediately suspended constitutional guarantees for 45 days. Political opponents and suspected revolutionaries were arrested and detained without charges; the press was censored and newspapers were prevented from printing editorials. The *New York Times* described the period as "The Great Silence."

Fidel's wife Mirta knew nothing of the planned attack and learned of it only after it happened. Still, she used her family contacts to have the Archbishop of Santiago plead for Fidel's life before his military captors. His lover, Naty, knew more and, in fact, helped with the drafts of Fidel's "Moncada Manifesto."

The trial of those charged with the attacks upon the Moncada and Bayamo Army Barracks commenced on September 21, 1953, at the same Santiago Palace of Justice seized nearly two months earlier by Raúl Castro, Lester Rodríguez, and their men. As a lawyer, Fidel received permission to defend himself. After admitting his role in planning and executing the attacks, Fidel quickly turned the tables against the government by asserting that the Batista regime had closed all avenues of legitimate protest since the March 10, 1952, coup d'état that brought him to power. On the second day of the trial, Fidel brought to the stand a parade of witnesses who testified about the executions and torture inflicted by Batista's army upon those captured since July 26. On both occasions Fidel enhanced his presentations with the oratory skills he learned as a student and with theatrics that included wearing the lawyer's robe when in that role and returning to civilian clothes when a defendant. On the third day of the trial, September 26, Fidel was conspicuously absent. His military guardians claimed that Fidel was ill, a charge quickly refuted by Raúl Castro and Melba Hernández, the latter presenting a personal letter written by Fidel the night before. In it, Castro claimed that his captors intended to assassinate him. Although the judges visited Castro in his cell and found him in good health and spirits, the military refused to dispatch him to court. The whole affair became public knowledge across Cuba, transmitted by word of mouth from those Santiagoans who attended the trial, and by Marta Rojas, a writer for *Bohemia* and the only reporter to cover the entire trial.

For the remainder of the accused, the trial went on until October 5, 1953, when the court pronounced guilty the 26 men and 2 women who actually took part in the Moncada and Bayamo raids. Raúl and 2 others received 13-year sentences, 20 received 10 years in prison and 3 received 3-year sentences. The men served their time at the Presidio Modelo on the Isle of Pines. The two women, Melba Hernández and Haydeé Santamaría, each received 7-month sentences to be served at the Guanajay women's prison.

Fidel Castro's guilt was a foregone conclusion when his trial resumed on October 16th in the nurses' lounge at Santiago's Civic Hospital. Marta Rojas was again present. Again Castro spoke in his own defense. According to Rojas, for two hours Castro spoke from a series of notes. Initially, Castro justified the attacks on the cruelties of the Batista regime and called for the restoration of the 1940 constitution. Turning to socioeconomic issues, Castro called for a land distribution program for the rural poor and a more equitable distribution for urban workers. He also rejected the notion of a free market economy dominated by foreigners. He called upon the Cuban people to proceed with a revolution to achieve these goals, and should he die before the revolution succeeded, Castro asserted that "History will absolve me." Just as Karl Marx's *Manifesto* faded from popular view in 1848, so, too, did Castro's Manifesto in 1953. He was sentenced to 15 years in prison on the Isle of Pines. The realities of Cuban life in 1953—political oppression, economic hardship, and social stagnation—preoccupied the minds of the Cuban people, not the tirade of a would-be imprisoned revolutionary.

Despite his imprisonment, Castro did not go away. *Bohemia* magazine recognized Fidel as one of the 12 outstanding people of the year 1953, along with the Shah of Iran, Costa Rican President José Figueres, England's Queen Elizabeth, Soviet KGB chief Lavrenti Beria, and Cuban prize fighter Kid Gavilán.

Until his release from prison on May 15, 1955, in a general amnesty, Castro occupied himself at the Presidio Modelo by conducting classes on history and philosophy for his fellow revolutionaries, reading extensively, revising his "History will absolve me" speech, and writing letters to persons on the outside. Despite Castro's enthusiasm, his courtyard classroom was filled with mostly apathetic students, some semiliterate, others bored by the monotony of prison life, and still others more concerned with their futures. Castro's ferocious reading appetite included a broad spectrum of books sent to him by his wife, Mirta, and lover, Naty. At times, he claimed to have read up to 13 hours a day. His reading list included such works as Lenin's *State and Revolution*; Karl Marx's *Civil Wars in France*; A. J. Cronin's *Keys of the Kingdom* and *The Citadel*; Dostoevksi's *The Brothers Karamazov*; and Somerset Maugham's *The Razor's Edge* to mention only a few. Castro also asked his friends to send him all the information available on U.S. President Franklin D. Roosevelt, particularly his policies regarding agricultural and industrial expansion, taxation, wages, and programs for the underprivileged. Through it all, Castro began to develop a sociopolitical philosophy predicated on class conflict. Castro concluded that political ideology could be used as a practical tool in the service of those who made historic achievements.

Castro continued to dream of a Cuba in revolt against the Batista dictatorship. Following the release of Melba Hernández and Haydeé Santamaría from prison in February 1954, Castro encouraged them to reconstitute his followers in Havana to again take up his cause. He could not accept their difficulty to do so in light of Batista's repressive regime. While imprisoned, Castro went through numerous drafts of his "History will absolve me" speech. He released it in bits and pieces to the two women and instructed them to have 100,000 copies printed and distributed across the island, but their limited funds meant that only 27,500 copies made it from the printing press. In its final form, Castro's "History will absolve me" speech contained five revolutionary proposals to correct Cuba's ills:

1. Return political power to the people and proclaim the 1940 constitution the law of the nation until such a time as the people wish to change it.
2. Give all tenant and subtenant farmers, lessees, sharecroppers, and squatters free and clear title to their lands of 150 acres or less.
3. All large industrial, mercantile, and mining enterprises, including the sugar mills, must share 30 percent of their profits with their workers.
4. Sugar planters must share 55 percent of all sugar production with all small tenant farmers who have been established for 3 or more years.

5. The government should confiscate all holdings and all ill-gotten
    gains of those who had committed frauds during previous
    regimes, as well as the holdings and ill-gotten gains of all heirs.

Some analysts argue that they were precursors of what came after 1959,
but Castro said nothing at the time. Clearly, the distribution of "History
will absolve me" across Cuba in 1954 contributed to Batista's distaste for
Castro.

Fidel's personal life also deteriorated while imprisoned. For the first
year of Fidel's incarceration, his wife, Mirta, and his half-sister, Lidia, visited him regularly at the Isle of Pines and, on the outside, worked together
to keep his political network alive. He wrote to both of them regularly, as
he did to Naty Revuelta. While Revuelta was financially secure in her
marriage, Mirta Castro was not and accepted a *botello* in the Ministry of
the Interior. Set up by her brother Rafael, a subsecretary in the ministry,
Mirta received $90 a month for a job she did not work. Fidel knew noth-
ing of it until she was dismissed in July 1954. Apparently ignorant of her
economic plight, Castro failed to understand how she could accept such a
position and wrote his friend Luis Conte Agüero that the entire affair was
designed to embarrass Castro before the Cuban people. His appeal to
Mirta was to no avail. On July 24, she filed for divorce from Castro and
sent their son, Fidelito, to live with her family, the Díaz-Balarts.

As the depressed Fidel Castro sat in the Presidio Modelo, Fulgencio
Batista won the rigged presidential election in November 1954, leaving
opposition political groups in disarray. Inaugurated on February 24, 1955,
for a four-year term, Batista was lulled into a sense of self-confidence when
Vice President Richard Nixon visited the island earlier that month. The
visit left the popular impression that the United States approved of the
Batista regime. To assuage the Cuban sugar planters, Batista struck a sugar
deal with the Soviet Union; to mollify the working class, he initiated a
massive public works program. Batista also was under pressure from several amnesty groups to release political prisoners. His advisors concurred,
thinking that it would help squelch the smoldering political discontent.
On May 7, 1955, Batista signed a blanket amnesty. Eight days later, Fidel
Castro returned to Havana to a triumphant welcome.

If Batista believed that amnesty would quiet the opposition, he was
wrong, particularly with regard to Castro. On the ferry boat home he obtained pledges of support to continue his movement secretly and after-
ward continued the organizational work. In a press conference upon his
arrival in Havana, and in his many subsequent interviews, Castro promised to continue the struggle. But not all of the *Moncadanistas* remained

loyal to Fidel. Led by Orlando Castro (no relation to Fidel) and Raúl Martínez Arará, they believed that Castro's time had passed. Disappointed, but not discouraged, Fidel took to carving out his own niche. Beginning on May 19, he commenced a series of radio attacks on the Batista regime and also wrote a daily column for *La Calle* detailing the tortures inflicted upon the *Moncadanistas* by Batista's soldiers.

The violence against the regime and Batista's retaliation made Cuba an increasingly uncomfortable home for Fidel. In fact, his brother Raúl was the first to feel the pain. In June 1955, he and 26 others were charged with conspiring with former President Prío against the regime and Raúl, in particular, with planning to bomb the La Tosca movie theater. Raúl evaded the police and found refuge in the Mexican embassy, where he was given political asylum and safe passage out of the country.

Amidst these cross currents, Fidel persuaded the leadership of the old MNR—Rafael García Bárcena, Armando Hart, Faustino Pérez, and Frank País—to join forces with Castro's own movement. País would prove to be the most important of the group.

With Raúl in Mexico and Batista again cracking down on dissidents, Fidel decided that he too must leave the island. Now divorced from Mirta, he asked Naty Revuelta to accompany him to Mexico, where he promised to marry her. She refused. Again alone, and with the financial assistance of his parents and his sister Lidia, Fidel Castro departed for Mexico on July 7, 1955. From Mexico, he sent a press release back to Havana in which he advised that all the doors for a peaceful resolution of the country's political crisis had been closed and, like José Martí before him, Castro promised to continue the fight on behalf of the Cuban people.

Mexico City long served as a haven for Cuban exiles and expatriates seeking refuge from the uncertainties of life on the island. Maria Antonia González de Poloma was one such person. She provided meals for the near destitute Castro brothers for some time after their arrival in Mexico City, as did *Ortodoxo* leader Juan Orta Cardona, and Moncada and Bayamo veterans residing in the capitol. Fidel also established relationships with potential financial benefactors, such as Orlando de Cárdenas and Alfonso "Fofo" Gutiérrez. A native Cuban, Cárdenas resided in Mexico for nearly a generation as a permanent resident. Gutiérrez was a successful Mexican engineer.

In August 1955, Fidel persuaded Colonel Alberto Bayo, for a monthly salary of $80, to train Castro's army. A Cuban native who served in the Republican Army during the Spanish Civil War in the 1930s, Bayo traveled between apartments where the rebels resided in Mexico City. While Castro used his charm and rhetoric to persuade his benefactors, he imposed harsh discipline upon his recruits who arrived from Cuba alone or in pairs. By summer's end, 60 to 70 men resided in rented houses and apartments scattered throughout Mexico City. As in the days preceding the Moncada attack, Castro organized his 26th of July Movement in cell-like fashion.

At some point in July, Castro met with Argentinean Ernesto "Che" Guevara. For 10 hours they spoke at the home of their mutual friend, Maria Antonia González, also a Cuban émigré. Guevara, a trained medical doctor, understood the grotesque socioeconomic disparities and restrictive political systems that gripped most of Latin America. Guevara was quickly taken in by Castro's charm and persuasiveness and accepted the Cuban's invitation to join the rebel cause as its physician.

Still, by October 1955, owing to a shortage of funding, Castro had made little material progress. That month he set out for the United States. Like José Martí before him, Castro appealed to the Cuban communities in Miami, Key West, and Tampa, Florida; Philadelphia; Union City, New Jersey; Bridgeport, Connecticut; and New York City, among others. He identified with the Cubans who left the island to escape political corruption, Batista's brutality, and the plight of the workingman. Significantly, to his New York audience, Castro vowed to return to the island in 1956. Just how much money Castro collected remains unknown. Estimates range from just enough to cover the cost of his trip to several thousands of dollars.

As Castro plotted in Mexico City, he also maintained contact with his followers in Havana, mostly through Melba Hernández. Castro was pleased to learn that his followers had seized control of the *Ortodoxo* National Congress on August 16, 1955. Before a packed auditorium, Faustino Pérez, Armando Hart, and Maria Laborte marched to the platform in the middle of a session to read Castro's message from Mexico calling for a revolution. In the emotion of the day, the *Fidelistas* pushed through a resolution endorsing a revolution as the only means to bring about change in Cuba. The party elders subsequently rejected the resolution, but it set in motion a confrontation between Fulgencio Batista and the Cuban youth.

Despite the boldness of the *Ortodoxo* youth, Castro's group was one of many active elements working against the Batista regime. Across the island, bombings and other acts of destruction, workers' slowdowns, meetings and demonstrations, and mimeographed fly sheets all signaled the extent of discontent with the government. Among the most visible groups was the Directorio Revolucionario (DR), an offshoot of the University of Havana's student government headed by José Antonio Echevarría. Although the DR also promoted an insurrectionary response to the Batista administration, it refused to merge with Castro's 26th of July Movement. The majority of the university students had distanced themselves from Castro.

A group of young army officers led by Colonel Ramón Barquín and supported by Justo Carrillo's *Montecristo* movement attempted a coup d'état on April 4, 1956. If successful, Carrillo was to become president. Instead, Batista learned of the plot in advance. As a result, Barquín went off to prison and Carrillo came to support Castro's cause.

Throughout 1956 the Dominican Republic's strongman, Rafael Trujillo, supported Batista's opponents, including former President Prío, in their attempts to oust Batista. Rumors suggested that Trujillo planned an invasion of Cuba, something he consistently denied. Batista was aware of the linkage. Although the invasion never materialized, Batista did all he could to discredit Castro by including him among the plotters.

In addition to those advocating violence, others sought political compromise with Batista. The Sociedad de Amigos de la República (SAR) became the most important group. Founded in 1955, this nonpartisan organization headed by Cosme de la Torriente, sponsored mass public rallies to demand new elections that forced Batista into talks with Torriente and other opposition figures, including moderate *Ortodoxos,* to devise a formula for new elections. The movement collapsed in March 1956 when Batista's delegates refused to consider a proposal for elections that same year. Castro's supporters rallied in opposition to SAR's efforts and when the dialogue collapsed, Torriente and others blamed Castro.

Castro understood that these machinations in Cuba militated against his ability to control events and, therefore, contributed to his desire to accelerate his return to the island. Planning for the invasion began in earnest in January 1956. The need for additional funding increased concomitantly. Under these circumstances Castro accepted the advice of Justo Carrillo and approached former President Prío. The two met clandestinely in the Casa Las Palmas Hotel in McAllen, Texas. The site was chosen because Prío, under federal investigation, could not leave the United States. Castro, also under surveillance by Mexican authorities and Cuban agents, surreptitiously made his way across the Rio Grande River with a group of Mexican laborers. Prío committed $50,000 to Castro's cause, $25,000 of it immediately. Carrillo gave another $5,000 and the Mexican engineer "Fofo" Gutiérrez and his friends advanced unaccounted sums. Newly purchased arms were stored in the safe houses and apartments around Mexico City and in the homes of Gutiérrez, Cárdenas, and Teresa Casuso, another Cuban exile residing in Mexico City.

In April 1956, Colonel Bayo, posing as a representative of an El Salvadoran military officer, arranged to rent a 60-square-mile ranch 25 miles outside of Mexico City. The rebel forces, along with the arms and munitions, were brought to Las Rosas, where military training, including guerrilla warfare, intensified. All the while, Castro exhorted his followers in Cuba to prepare for a nationwide uprising to coincide with his return.

Castro's activities did not go unnoticed by Mexican authorities, who increasingly saw Castro as an irritant, or to the Cuban intelligence agents in Mexico with orders to assassinate the revolutionary. Castro cleverly avoided both by constantly moving about and never sleeping more than one night in the same location. All went well until the evening of June 21, 1956, when Castro and five others were arrested by Mexican authorities and charged with violation of Mexican immigration laws by conspiring to organize a revolution against a foreign government and for the illegal possession of arms. Under interrogation, the Mexicans learned of the Las Rosas training center, which they subsequently raided. Forty-five more Cubans and Che Guevara were brought into custody. The Cuban embassy placed an article in Mexican City newspapers about the capture of "Cuban communists" linked in a revolutionary plot with former President Prío. In hopes of discrediting Castro in Cuba, a Mexican journalist sympathetic to Batista repeated the charges in an article written especially for *Bohemia*. In Mexico City, Castro quickly denied the allegations and, with a follow-up article, refuted the charges in *Bohemia*. Save for Che Guevara, who was detained another month, Castro and his men were released from prison on July 25. Former Mexican President Lazaro Cardenas, sympathetic to Castro's cause, intervened with the Mexican government to prevent his deportation.

Following his release, Castro accelerated his invasion plans. In late September 1956 he brought the 26th of July Movement leaders to Mexico. Not all were convinced that the time was appropriate for Castro to invade the island, but knowing that Castro could not be persuaded they offered little resistance, save Frank País, commander of Oriente Province and the location Castro intended for his landing. Desirous of a nationwide strike to accompany his invasion, Castro sought out communist leaders because of their influence over labor. In Mexico City, Castro met with Oswaldo Sánchez, who like Frank País, argued that more time was needed to prepare for such an action. In October, Melba Hernández returned from Cuba to advise Castro to delay because the 26th of July Movement leadership was in disarray and not yet prepared for a nationwide uprising. Angered at Castro's insistence to carry out his invasion in December 1956, Hernández warned him of repeating the Moncada tragedy. Castro fumed, but he was not deterred. Plans for the invasion at Oriente continued.

All did not go well. Castro's agents in Baltimore, Maryland placed a $5,000 down payment on a ship that he planned to place under Panamanian registry. He could not do so until the ship was paid for and, to sail out of U.S. waters, the owner was required to be a U.S. citizen. The Cuban embassy in Washington, D.C., learned of the pending sale and reported it to the Federal Bureau of Investigation (FBI). As the FBI investigated the sale, Castro abandoned the plan and the $5,000 down payment. Castro's agent in Tuxpan, Mexico, Antonio Conde, with little cash down and a personal mortgage, purchased the 58-foot *Granma* for $15,000 from a U.S. physician and, for another $10,000, a house in Tuxpan to be used as the revolutionary's assembly point. The poorly conditioned *Granma* underwent an extensive, but necessary, overhaul in order to be seaworthy for its sail to Cuba. Tuxpan appeared a good choice as a point of departure. The coastal town was too small to warrant a customs or immigration officer.

As training continued in Jalapa, Boca del Río, and Ciudad Victoria in Tamaulipas State, Castro was betrayed by his longtime friend and bodyguard, Rafael del Pino. He was secretly selling information to the Mexican authorities and when Castro became suspicious, del Pino sought protection from them. His revelations led to a raid on November 21 upon the home of Teresa Casuso and the discovery of countless arms and ammunition that Castro had stored next door. Fearing attacks upon his other installations, Castro ordered his men to make their way to the recently purchased safe house in Tuxpan. Castro remained in Cuernavaca until the last moment.

Throughout his stay in Mexico, Castro's private life continued its pattern of disappointments. On March 18, 1956, his former mistress in Havana, Naty Revuelta gave birth to a girl, Alina. The baby was Fidel's, not Naty's husband's, and most of Naty's social circle suspected the truth. Fidel dismissed the occasion. While meeting with his revolutionary planners on October 21, Castro received a telegram that his father had died. Again, he showed no emotion and refused to discuss the situation with his colleagues. Also, in mid-October, Castro's former wife, Mirta, who was planning her second marriage to a successful Cuban businessman, assented to Fidel's request that their son, Fidelito, visit his father in Mexico City for two weeks. Despite promises to the contrary, Castro did not intend to return his son to the Díaz-Balarts. He arranged for Fidelito to live with the Alfonso Gutiérrez family and promised to bring his son to Cuba upon the success of his revolution. Romance again entered Fidel's life but it exited soon after it began. Following his release from a Mexican prison on July 25, 1956, Castro met Isabelle Custodio, an attractive 18-year-old girl of Cuban-Spanish upper-class descent. Castro courted her and asked for her hand in marriage. Although the Custodio family agreed, it was not to be. Isabelle lost interest in going to Cuba as the nation's first lady. The courtship ended that October. Castro was too deeply involved in plotting the invasion at Oriente to fret too long over the rejection.

Following the raid on Teresa Casuso's home on November 21 by Mexican authorities, Castro learned that he had 72 hours to leave the country or face arrest. To ensure his own departure, Castro bribed officers in the immigration office. On the evening of November 24 he met up with his men at Tuxpan. For the first time, these would-be soldiers learned of their objective. Some questioned the wisdom of the plan, particularly when learning about the *Granma*. Castro attempted to assuage their doubt by asserting that 50,000 well-trained insurgents awaited their arrival and that workers nationwide would implement a general strike. None of this was true. In fact, Castro failed to inform the Revolutionary Directorate in Havana of his plans. But Batista knew he was coming. His agents in Cuba knew generally about Castro's plan and, on the eve of departure, the bribed immigration officers informed the Cuban Embassy in Mexico City that Castro was on his way home.

Amidst a heavy rain, 82 men, along with their arms, ammunition, and other supplies, crammed themselves upon the *Granma*, a vessel designed to hold only 12. Shortly after midnight, the overloaded *Granma* set sail for Cuba with only one engine running and no lights in order to reduce the possibility of being spotted by a Mexican naval vessel. The rains persisted for two days and, with the swollen seas, even Fidel pondered the potential success of the voyage as the ship missed its scheduled landing date of November 30. Out of contact with Fidel's entourage, Frank País proceeded, as planned, with coordinated attacks upon the Customs House, police headquarters, and harbor facilities in Santiago. This was to draw Batista's military forces away from Castro's designated landing site near Niquero and seize arms and munitions before fleeing to the Sierra Maestra. However, the Directorio and Communist labor leadership in Havana, awaiting further developments, did not call for a general uprising or nationwide strike.

The *Granma* finally reached Cuba on December 2. It actually ran aground, causing Castro and his 82 followers to wade through mangrove swamps to reach shore. Once there, a Cuban patrol boat began shelling the shoreline as helicopters and airplanes fired from above. As a result, Castro lost 42 men to death or capture and another 21 to desertion. With Batista's army in pursuit, the remainder struggled on their own to reach the farm of Ramón Pérez, the prearranged rendezvous point. By the end of December, 18 men, plus Fidel, survived the invasion. Castro's momentary disappearance from public view led the Cuban government to announce that his forces had been wiped out and that Castro had been killed. The announcement brought a sense of despair to the 26th of July Movement followers in Havana.

Their despondency disappeared when they learned of Castro's successful attack upon the isolated military garrison at La Plata on January 17 and five days later when his forces ambushed a government patrol, inflicting heavy casualties. Castro's success threatened Batista's confidence. He suspended civil rights, an action he hoped to use to ferret out revolutionaries, but an act that only stiffened the resistance to him.

Castro needed more. Although he remained optimistic and committed to the success of the revolution, the morale among his camp followers was low and his urban forces appeared in disarray. To gain momentum, he sent word to the 26th of July Movement leadership in Havana that he wished to meet with a U.S. journalist. They found Herbert Matthews, a *New York Times* reporter, anxious to take on the assignment. Matthews, a veteran correspondent who covered the Spanish Civil War in the 1930s, viewed the assignment as an opportunity to gain notoriety for himself, not so much for Castro.

Castro orchestrated the interview on February 17, 1957, in the Sierra Maestra. When the three part series appeared in the *Times* beginning February 27, complete with a photo of Matthews and Castro together, it gave the impression that the rebel army was far stronger than the 18 men Castro had in camp and that it had successfully engaged Batista's columns on several occasions. In reality, it had only two such encounters. The interview emphasized the nationalistic character of Castro's movement and his social intention for Cuba's future. Castro also railed against colonialism and imperialism but professed his friendship for the American people. Matthews incorrectly reported that an estimated 90 percent of the Cuban middle and upper social sectors supported Castro.

While the *Times* articles awakened the American public to Fidel Castro and generated some sympathy for his cause, their publication in Cuba caused real excitement. Cuban emotions were further elevated with the distribution of Castro's "Appeal to the Cuban People," which included a litany of charges against the Cuban government and a call for the violent overthrow of the Batista regime, beginning with the destruction of the country's economic base—the sugar cane fields. The "Appeal" offered nothing new. Castro had made similar statements in the past, all of which reflected his "History will absolve me" discourse during the 1953 trial for the Moncada Army Barracks raid.

Over the next several months Castro's band of forces grew as peasants in the Sierra Maestra, who had long endured the horrible working conditions on the sugar and cattle plantations and abuse from the local militia charged with keeping order in the countryside, joined the rebel cause. The peasants also knew the terrain, which proved very important in the successful raids upon the regular army. At the time, Castro appeared content with these actions and acts of sabotage. He was not yet ready for the final offensive, for which vast amounts of arms and munitions were needed. Funds for these acquisitions came from Cuban planters and ranchers in order to spare their crops and livestock from destruction, from the urban middle sector that anticipated more representative government once Batista was ousted, and from the exile community that funneled their support to Fidel through his sisters Emma and Lidia in Mexico City.

To counteract the peasant support for Castro, Batista's army resorted to indiscriminate terror. The army forced thousands of peasants into hastily constructed camps near Santiago and Bayamo, reminiscent of the Spanish *reconcentrados* during the Spanish-American War in 1898. As in 1898, the goal was to isolate the peasants from the rebels. The abhorrent conditions and treatment of the peasants in those camps only drove more of them into the rebel camp. Those not brought into the camps were presumed to be Castro supporters and were treated harshly, even executed. By mid-1957, a good portion of the Sierra Maestra was up in arms. Less than a year later, Raúl Castro operated a second front in the north, Juan Almeida led a third front around Santiago, Camilo Cienfuegos left the Sierra for the Holguín plains, and Che Guevara operated around Turquino peak.

In response to the events in Oriente, the faculty and students at the University of Havana voted to shut down the institution on November 30, 1957. It remained closed until after Castro marched into Havana in January 1959. The government's action only propelled the students into the nation's political dynamics with one goal: to end the Batista dictatorship. In an attack upon the presidential palace on March 13, 1957, a student group almost succeeded in killing Batista, but the students lost their leader, José Antonio Echevarría, who was killed in a coordinated attack upon a Havana radio station; he was the same Echevarría who, earlier, had refused to come under Castro's control. His death opened the door for new rebel leadership to unite rural and urban movements.

Castro capitalized upon Echevarría's death. Henceforth, he used his Havana-based supporters to coordinate the underground acts of sabotage and subversion. The rebels sought to disrupt the government at every turn and to show the Cuban people that the corrupt government could not protect its own interests and, by implication, had neither legitimacy nor claim on citizen's loyalty. The rebels exploded bombs, set fires, cut power lines, derailed trains, and kidnapped and killed their political enemies. Batista responded with equal ferocity with the indiscriminate torture and murder of Castro supporters, suspected or real. The violence also led to a series of planned military uprisings against the government. Beginning in April 1956, army officers, then naval officers at Cienfuegos, and later, the air force and army medical corps, conspired to change governments.

In March 1958, Batista refused to accept a proposal from the Joint Committee on Civic Institutions. The committee was an umbrella for 42 middle sector organizations, which, along with the Catholic Bishops, proposed that Batista resign and accept a coalition government. These groups were drawn to Castro by his promise to replace the Batista dictatorship with a democratic government. They did not see Castro as a possible, or even fledgling, communist in the spring of 1958. By the middle of 1958, Batista not only faced mounting popular opposition, but also an increasingly disloyal and unreliable military. Batista became more and more isolated.

As a result of the rural insurgency and urban violence, by 1958 the Cuban economy stagnated, causing a drastic decline in government public works projects and a sharp rise in unemployment. Poverty became more visible in Havana and other cities. Petty crime and prostitution climbed. Batista's apparent indifference toward U.S. organized crime's control of vice and gambling further intensified the opposition against the regime. At the same time, Castro's rural guerrillas had inflicted a heavy toll. They halted the shipment of foodstuffs into the cities, causing prices to soar. Transportation between Havana and the three eastern provinces came to a virtual standstill. Telephone and telegraph service across the island was paralyzed. Large sections of highways and railroads were destroyed; and bridges were put out of service. Matters worsened in February when the 26th of July Movement launched an attack against sugar mills, tobacco factories, public utilities, railroads, and oil refineries and put the torch to some two million tons of sugar.

The urban-based opposition groups and, particularly, Faustino Pérez, long argued that a nationwide general strike would paralyze the country and, in turn, force Batista from office. Fidel accepted the idea but was unsure of the timing of its implementation. In early March 1958, when mediation efforts failed, Pérez visited with Castro in the Sierra Maestra where he convinced Castro that now was the time. The scheduled April 9 general strike failed miserably for a variety of reasons, including poor planning and communications, overconfidence, underestimation of the national police force's ability to react, and the failure to utilize communist organizations, largely due to Castro's dislike of them. But the strike's failure strengthened Castro's position. Pérez and other urban leaders were dismissed from their position and Castro was made commander in chief of all revolutionary forces of the 26th of July Movement.

Castro's strong position was apparent in July 1958, when representatives of eight opposition groups met in Caracas, Venezuela, including the 26th of July Movement and the student Directorio, but not the communists. As a result of the conclave, the participants agreed to create a revolutionary, civic coalition of all Cuban social sectors and to provide for a common strategy to defeat Batista by military means. To satiate the urban groups there was also an agreement to call for another general strike, but no date was set. They also agreed that a provisional government, headed by Manuel Urrutia, would replace Batista until a constitutional and democratic government could be established. The anticipated provisional government was charged with maintaining public order, including the punishment of those guilty of treason, protecting worker's rights, satisfying international obligations, and insuring the social and economic progress of all Cuban people. In one stroke, the Caracas Pact reflected the frustration of the rebel groups with the Batista regime and its appeal to the middle and lower socioeconomic groups. For Castro, whose military strength could not be questioned, the Caracas Pact enhanced his image as a moderate. The Caracas Pact also asked the United States to cease all military and other types of assistance to the Batista regime. But, that already had happened.

When the Eisenhower administration entered office in January 1953, Cuba appeared as a distant concern. At the time, the administration had little understanding of the depths of the opposition to Cuban President Fulgencio Batista. Eisenhower's first ambassador to Cuba, Arthur Gardner, was a political appointee and totally unprepared for the task before him. During his tenure, Gardner established very close relations with Batista and ignored the State Department's instructions to establish contact with Batista's leading political opponents. Gardner was not alone in his positive assessments of Batista. During his visit to Havana in February 1955, Vice President Richard M. Nixon publicly compared Batista with Abraham Lincoln. And to Eisenhower, Nixon described the Cuban leader as a remarkable man interested, not in himself, but in Cuba's socioeconomic development.

The embassy passed off Fidel Castro as an "ambitious and ruthless opportunist" for leading 182 followers in a raid upon the Moncada Army Barracks in Santiago de Cuba on July 26, 1953. Other than expressing relief when Castro was subsequently sentenced to a 15-year prison term, the embassy made no special note of the event. When Batista released Castro from prison in May 1955, Gardner failed to report to Washington the popular outburst of enthusiasm for Castro, nor Castro's pledge to continue the revolution from abroad. Throughout 1955 and 1956, Gardner ignored the significance or impact of the pro-Castro propaganda being distributed across the island and its promise that Castro would return to liberate the country from tyranny. Instead, Gardner believed that the Cubans were too prosperous and politically apathetic to be concerned with a would-be revolutionary. Significantly, Assistant Secretary of State, Henry Holland, concurred with Gardner's views. When the *New York Times* reporter Herbert Matthews met clandestinely with Castro in February 1957 and erroneously reported on the strength of the rebel army, Gardner spent his time pointing out the mistakes in Matthews' reporting, but said nothing about the size of the rebel army. He also neglected to report the elevation of Castro's prestige across Cuba as a result of the articles. Although Gardner now described Castro and his followers as socialists and nationalists who promised to transform Cuba, the ambassador did not see the impractical, possibly megalomaniac Castro as a threat to Batista. Assistant Secretary of State, Roy Rubottom, accepted Gardner's reports. In an October 1957 news conference Rubottom asserted that the mass majority of the Cuban people were satisfied with their quality of life. Only a few State Department and Central Intelligence Agency (CIA) analysts argued to the contrary. They concluded that Batista's position stood on weak legs, but these reports made no impact upon upper echelon policymakers.

Another financial contributor to the Republican Party and successful Wall Street financier without international experience, Earl E. T. Smith, replaced Gardner in June 1957. Mistrust characterized his relationship with the embassy staff and particularly the embassy's chief political officer, John Topping, which resulted in Smith's approval of all cables sent to Washington. Most analyses contrary to Smith's perception did not reach the State Department. At the same time, Smith feared public criticism from Secretary of State, John Foster Dulles, if he did not portray issues in Cuba within the Cold War context or was overly critical of Batista. Under these conditions, Smith was wary about criticizing Batista's regime. As Castro's position strengthened in late 1957 and throughout 1958, Smith became convinced that the rebel was a communist. As Batista's position weakened, the State Department encouraged Smith to meet with moderate opposition leaders in an effort to bring about a solution to the growing crisis. Smith refused, arguing that to do so constituted intervention in Cuba's internal affairs. For that reason, Smith sidestepped the March 1958 effort by the Joint Committee for Civic Institutions to reach a mediated end to the conflict.

If Gardner and Smith failed to pursue a proactive policy in Cuba, the Eisenhower administration in Washington did not. In March, it imposed an arms embargo upon the Cuban government because of its massive human rights violations, not out of sympathy for the revolution. Still, the United States continued to suffer a public relations problem. Under the terms of the 1948 Military Assistance Program (MAP) agreement, between 1952 and 1958 the United States supplied Cuba with $10 million in military hardware, including tanks, howitzers, armor piercing cartridges, semiautomatic rifles, hand grenades, and vintage World War II aircraft and bombs. Intended for use in the defense of the Caribbean region from an external attack, Batista instead used this matériel upon suspected revolutionary supporters, including civilians. If this were not enough to link the United States to Batista, an official visit to Havana by the aircraft carrier *Leyte* and the awarding of the United States Legion of Merit to Cuban Air Force Colonel Carlos M. Tabernilla y Palermo, sealed the image. At the same time, U.S. authorities labored to prevent the clandestine dispatch of matériel to Castro, but just how successful the effort was remains a matter of conjecture. The U.S. denial of arms to Batista in March 1958 was not only an effort to correct the publicity problem, but also to bring Batista to the negotiating table. It failed on both counts. Nor did the U.S. embargo prevent Batista from finding other sources of supply, particularly from European and Israeli arms merchants. Still, the imposition of the U.S. arms embargo boosted the rebels' confidence while deflating what little hope Batista's supporters had for U.S. assistance.

Following the failure of the April 9 general strike, Batista perceived a weakness in the opposition forces, particularly those following Fidel Castro. At the beginning of May, Batista sent 10,000 troops into Oriente Province to cordon off the Sierra Maestra and slowly tighten the circle around Castro's troops. In the process, his forces used remaining U.S. military equipment, including bombs, all of which left the popular impression that the U.S. continued to support the Cuban dictator. Batista's offensive fizzled after 76 days. His military had engaged in 30 clashes ranging from major battles to small skirmishes. In the process, the morale and skill of the rebel troops increased, at the same time the national army morale dwindled. In fact, many of the army deserted and joined the rebel forces. On August 7, Batista's demoralized and beaten army pulled out of the Sierra Maestra. They would not return.

As the fighting ensued Ambassador Smith saw only two choices— Batista or Castro. To Smith, Batista defended U.S. business interests on the island, whereas Castro promised their demise.

By August the Cuban situation was extremely fluid. Amid the worsening economic conditions, reports of graft, corruption, and Swiss bank accounts opened by Batista and his supporters added to the public outrage and fueled the popular determination to oust the dictator from power. The weakness of national military prompted some of Batista's supporters to remove him as a way to cool tensions and, they hoped, to appease the various rebel groups. The movement for change was now irreversible and it favored the bold.

Castro took the bold step. In August 1958, Castro's forces commenced what came to be their final offensive. Castro intended to surround the major cities, Santiago, Santa Clara, and Havana, and sever the national transportation system. In late August the offensive began, and by the end of October the national rail and road lines were cut. In the fighting that continued, Batista's forces offered little resistance and, in fact, withdrew from the battlefield. Castro's forces controlled numerous small towns and almost all military outposts in the interior.

By November 1958 the State Department and the CIA lost all confidence in Ambassador Smith's reports from Havana. Instead, both agencies foresaw Castro's potential victory, unless a mediated solution could be found. It would not be Rivero Agüero, Batista's handpicked successor who won the rigged November 1958 presidential election, an election in which most voters abstained.

In a meeting at the State Department on November 22, 1958, Smith remained insistent on the choices before U.S. policymakers—Batista or Castro. The State Department thought otherwise. Department officials understood that Batista had lost all support, yet they were suspicious of Castro's intentions. The State Department wanted to replace Batista with a moderate figure. Toward that objective, and with Eisenhower's approval, they dispatched William Pawley on a mission to Havana in early December 1958. Smith learned of the mission through his Cuban contacts, not the State Department. Pawley, a Republican businessman long connected to Cuba, was not authorized to present himself as a representative of the Eisenhower administration, but rather to explain that he came as a private U.S. citizen representing influential friends in the United States. He offered Batista and his family safe haven in Florida, on the condition that Batista form a caretaker government acceptable to Washington, which would then turn on the military assistance spigot in order to prevent a Castro victory. Batista refused. Even if Batista had accepted the offer, it might have come too late. Without support within Cuba and cut off from the United States, Batista fled the country for the Dominican Republic in the early hours of January 1, 1959.

Before leaving, Batista turned the power of government over to the Chief of Cuba's Joint General Staff and military commander of Oriente Province, General Eulogio Cantillo. But his position was immediately weakened when, at the same time, Castro secured the release of Colonel Ramón Barquín—who had engineered the failed coup d'état in 1956 by moderate officers—from the Isle of Pines prison. Proclaiming to be commander in chief of Cuba's armed forces, Barquín telephoned Castro in Santiago to ask when Manuel Urrutia would assume the presidency. He would have to wait. For the moment, the revolutionaries, of which Fidel Castro was the most recognizable, had severed Cuba from its past.

For a while on January 1, 1959, an eerie silence fell over Havana, as its residents boarded up their homes and remained inside fearing violence and looting in the absence of any government. When it did not immediately happen, the Cubans returned to the streets to celebrate the Batista's ouster. By the evening, however, the looting and destruction began, lasting well into the night of January 2 when Castro's rebel forces marched into the city and restored order.

Meanwhile in front of the Moncada Army Barracks in Santiago, Fidel Castro announced the formation of a new government with Urrutia as the popularly elected provisional president. In Mexico City, Castro's friend and supporter Teresa Casuso walked to the Cuban embassy and installed herself as ambassador of Urrutia's Revolutionary Government. The Mexican authorities quickly extended recognition. In Washington, D.C., Ernesto Betancourt, a representative of Castro's 26th of July Movement, walked into the Cuban embassy, where, along with some of his friends, he took over the chancery and ousted the sitting ambassador. The United States did not immediately extend recognition. At the Pentagon, the Naval Chief of Staff, Admiral Arleigh Burke argued that the United States must take some action to prevent Castro from seizing control of Cuba. The Eisenhower administration decided against the only option immediately available—dispatching the marines to Cuba.

Castro took a meandering route from Santiago to Havana to ensure his visibility before as many Cubans as possible. He finally arrived in Havana on January 8 to a euphoric welcome. His charisma would prove to be overwhelming. Fidel and his followers called themselves the generation of the century, based on the date of José Martí's birth (1853) and the attack on Moncada (1953). The *Fidelistas* claimed they came to invoke history and, therefore, would install a Cuban democratic government and social justice. The structures of the old Cuba were to be dismantled and, in its place, a new Cuba created.

In six years, Fidel Castro moved from a wild-eyed would-be revolutionary when he led the attack upon the Moncada Army Barracks in 1953, to a liberating hero who saved Cuba from dictatorship and corruption when he marched into Havana on January 8, 1959. Despite the transformation and the accompanying publicity, Castro remained an enigma. No one really understood him or what he stood for.

Chapter 3

THE RUSSIANS ARE COMING

During the first week of January 1959, as Castro meandered across the island en route from Santiago to Havana, stopping to greet everyone along the way and granting interviews to foreign journalists including a taped session for the popular U.S. Sunday evening Ed Sullivan television show, *Fidelista* troops, led by Che Guevara and Camilo Cienfuegos, restored order to Havana. Castro arrived in Havana on January 8, atop a tank, along with his son, Fidelito, who had been flown in from Long Island, New York, where he had been living during the last stages of the Revolution. An estimated three million people greeted Castro as he made his way to the Presidential Palace. He presented a brief nationalistic speech promising a new Cuba. When a group of doves were released, one found a home on Fidel's shoulder as he spoke to the crowd. The symbol fit his charisma. Castro was an instant hero. He then moved into the twenty-second floor of the Havana Hilton, which he quickly renamed the Havana Libre. His staff and security people occupied the two floors immediately below.

Castro and his entourage arrived in Havana unprepared to govern. Manuel Urrutia was president, José Miró Cardona prime minister, and Fidel, commander in chief. They had no plans for creating a new government out of the chaos Batista left behind, nor did they understand the intricacies of economic policies. But, clearly, Castro wanted power and control. While having dinner on the evening of January 1, 1959, at the La Covadonga Restaurant in Santiago with leaders of the Second Escambray front, Castro reportedly said that he intended to dispatch Che Guevara to the Dominican Republic, where hopefully he would lose his life in the effort to topple the dictator Rafael Trujillo. Raúl, Fidel's brother, was to be sent to Europe as some type of roving ambassador. True or not, Castro's comments confirm his established pattern of eliminating any threats to his authority. Che and Raúl were never banished, but soon Castro took to eliminating his opposition.

President Urrutia negotiated with the leadership of the DR, Faure Chomón and Rolando Cubela, to vacate the National Palace so that neither was present when Castro addressed the crowd shortly after his arrival on January 8. Castro went further that evening when, before another large crowd, he denounced the DR for seizing arms from the Cuban military with the intention of using them to thwart the Revolution. In the process, Castro stirred the crowd into chanting against the DR. He effectively emasculated them.

More ominous were the summary trials and execution by firing squad of *Batistianos* and other so-called enemies of the Revolution. In Camagüey on January 5, while en route to Havana, Castro directed his provincial military commanders to commence summary court martials of war criminals, officers and lower-ranking military personnel, policeman, and others accused of torturing and killing unarmed civilians and members of the revolutionary forces. The origins of the directive rested in a February 11, 1958, decree Castro issued while in the Sierra Maestra. Raúl Castro wasted no time. In Santiago, in the same room that the *Moncadistas* had been tried in 1953, Raúl immediately orchestrated the trial and execution of 70 such accused people, the last of which was filmed and aired on U.S. television. The Americans reacted in horror and some in disbelief that Fidel Castro was associated with the atrocities. Fidel fumed. The reaction only confirmed his belief that the Americans failed to comprehend the tyranny endured by the Cubans and that such war criminals deserved their fate. How could they ignore the estimated 20,000 deaths and disappearances carried out by the Batista regime? Castro asked.

The trials continued. In fact, they took on a public face. Crowds estimated as high as 17,000 gathered in Havana's stadium or witnessed the trials on national television. Many of Batista's henchmen, like Major Jesús Sosa Blanco, met their fate in proceedings Castro likened to the Nuremburg Trials of the Nazi leadership at the end of World War II. Others were convicted on less substantive evidence; young children asserted that the accused raped their mothers and sisters and that they overworked and did not pay their fathers. This was enough testimony to put one before the firing squad. In the first six months of 1959, approximately 550 were executed by firing squad amidst calls of *paredón!* (to the wall). The international outcry slowed the pace of the trials, but did not end them.

Castro also turned on his supporters. For example, after a court in Santiago acquitted 43 airmen for bombing the rebel forces, Castro denounced the verdict on television and demanded their retrial. As a result, the men, all of whom made no effort to flee the island and declared their loyalty to Castro, received 30-year prison sentences. Hubert Matos, one of Fidel's most successful commanders, questioned the direction of the revolution in October 1959 and for so doing was sentenced to 30 years in prison. The executions and prison sentences served notice throughout all of Cuban society not to question the revolutionary leadership. The executions and imprisonments were an extension of Castro's determination to be in control.

In early 1959, as public attention focused upon the trials and executions of the Revolution's opponents, the Cuban government was restructured. President Urrutia, considered a moderate, formed a new cabinet that consisted largely of anti-Batista figures who came from the upper and middle classes. Most were competent individuals. Next, through a series of decrees, Urrutia oversaw the dissolution of congress; the removal from office of all congressmen, provincial governors, mayors, and municipal councilman; and a widespread purge of pro-Batista supporters in the government bureaucracy. Prior to Castro's departure for the United States in April 1959, the Revolution was taking on a new shape. The traditional *Auténtico* and *Ortodoxo* political parties were isolated. By March 1959, Castro was emerging as the center of Cuba's political life.

The events within Cuba increased American interest and puzzlement about Fidel Castro and led to an invitation from the American Society of Newspaper Editors to address their convention in Washington in April 1959. Castro arrived in Washington, D.C., on April 15, 1959, to begin an 11-day tour of the eastern United States and Canada. President Dwight D. Eisenhower chose not to meet with Castro, and conveniently absented himself from Washington. On April 16, Castro lunched with Acting Secretary of State, Christian A. Herter; on April 19 he met for two hours with Vice President Richard M. Nixon; and, on April 20 Castro spoke informally with members of the Senate Foreign Relations and House Foreign Affairs Committees. En route to New York, on April 20 Castro stopped at Princeton University to meet with students and meet privately with former Secretary of State Dean Acheson.

In his April 17 address before the American Society of Newspaper Editors Castro reiterated that: (1) his regime had executed only those guilty of war crimes; (2) he had no intention of abrogating the 1934 treaty that guaranteed the U.S. rights to the Guantánamo Naval Base; (3) Cuba would remain a member of the Inter-American Mutual Defense Pact; (4) Cuba would not confiscate private industry and, in fact, encouraged further foreign investment; and (5) Cuba did not want U.S. aid, but welcomed additional trade opportunities.

Castro made other major pronouncements. On April 19, during an interview on NBC-TV's *Meet the Press*, Castro denied statements attributed to him that Cuba would remain neutral in the event of a conflict between the United States and the Soviet Union. Affirming previous commitments to democracy, Castro promised that free elections would be held in Cuba within four years. Before the National Press Club in Washington, D.C., on April 20, Castro said that agrarian reform was the next step to be taken in the Cuban Revolution. Uncultivated or badly cultivated land would be legally expropriated to create an internal market and provide employment for approximately 700,000 people.

Castro also visited New York City from April 21 to 23, Boston on April 25, and Montreal, Canada on April 26. In his public speeches throughout the trip, Castro professed friendship for the United States, reiterated his promise for elections in no more than four years and belittled the charges of communist influence in his government.

Instead of returning directly to Havana, Castro flew to Buenos Aires, Argentina, where he addressed the Organization of American States (OAS) Social and Economic Council. He proposed the creation of a Latin American Common Market and called upon the United States to implement a 10-year $30 million aid package for Latin America. Reportedly, a Fidel assistant Ernesto Betancourt, who eventually defected to the United States, coined the phrase "Alliance for Progress" that President John F. Kennedy would use three years later in launching a U.S. assistance program.

Although the trip appeared as a public relations success, Castro returned to Havana disappointed; he had received no credit for overthrowing the despicable Batista regime and there was a lack of interest in the social goals he had for the Cuban people. He found the Americans interested only in learning that neither he nor his Revolution had communist leanings.

Castro also returned home with his zeal to keep the spirit of the Revolution alive, to make decisions which, although immensely popular in the short term, would prove economically disastrous later on. These decisions also reflected Fidel's inexperience and lack of understanding of basic economics.

Unlike the victors in most civil wars, Castro inherited a relatively healthy economy in 1959. Sugar prices were low but stable and, with the start of the sugar harvest season, unemployment was at a minimum. Foreign investment in the country was substantial, with an estimated $1.2 billion from the United States alone. Stores were filled with consumer goods, and tourists, particularly attracted by the widespread gambling and prostitution, maintained a constant flow of foreign exchange into the country. The revolutionary war against Batista had done relatively little harm to the economy.

Castro made two decisions in the spring of 1959 that reflected his revolutionary zeal and also his lack of understanding economics. The decisions signaled the Revolution's future direction. The first came in March 1959, prior to his departure for the United States. At his direction, the Cuban government implemented the Urban Reform Law designed to discourage investments in real estate and construction of private dwellings. The law decreed a 50 percent reduction in rents less than $100 monthly, a 40 percent reduction for rents between $100 and $200, and a 30 percent reduction for those more than $200. The newly established Instituto Nacional Ahorros y Vivienda (INAV) acquired vacant lots upon which it pledged to construct inexpensive public housing.

The second signal, agrarian reform, mentioned during his April 19 interview on NBC's *Meet the Press*, became a reality on May 17, 1959, with the Agrarian Reform Law. It restricted real estate holdings to 1,000 acres—except for sugar, rice, and livestock farms, the staples of Cuba's agricultural economy. In the latter, maximum limits were set at 3,333 acres. Estates above these amounts were nationalized with compensation provided at 4.5 percent in 25-year bonds based upon the values declared in the 1948 tax records, which were notoriously undervalued. The bonds were never issued. The expropriated lands were reorganized into state cooperatives or distributed into individual holdings of 67 acres with squatters, sharecroppers, and renters receiving first claim to the land they had been working. When the United States protested the law's compensation provisions, Castro concluded that there could be no accommodation with Washington.

The law also created the Instituto Nacional de la Reforma Agraria (INRA), with Fidel Castro as its director. Initially designed to supervise the land distribution program, Castro gave it new meaning and, for him, a source of publicity and power, as it took on responsibility for road construction, housing programs, health facilities, and educational projects. Effectively, Castro made President Urrutia and the cabinet less important in the decision-making process.

With the announcement of the Agrarian Reform Law on May 17, 1959, Cuba embarked on a new path. The new Cuba, Castro proclaimed, would focus upon full employment, expanded health care, extended education, and the need to create a new political consciousness among the people. Elections, he argued, would only interfere with these programs. Castro's promise to abide by the 1940 Constitution and hold elections faded away and, with it, the concomitant privileges of Cuba's upper and middle classes.

In the following months, the Cuban government intervened in the telephone and electric companies, lowering their rates. Virtually all wage contracts were rewritten, with the laborers receiving 15 percent increases. Unemployment relief followed. Health and education reforms were introduced, particularly in the rural areas. Property owned by all past government officials, senior army officers, mayors, governors, and members of congress for the 1954–58 time period was confiscated. Through special licensing and higher tariffs, the importation of luxury items, including cars and television sets, was restricted. Although largely symbolic, the measures helped to curb the Cuban appetite for U.S. goods. It saved the loss of an estimated $70 million in foreign exchange the first year and reduced trade with the United States from $224 million in 1959 to $34 million in 1960. Although most of these programs were popular among the masses of Cuban people, they also contributed to the draining of the public treasury. The Cuban economy and national treasury were further battered by the loss of sugar income because of a drop in world prices and a steep decline in the tourist industry brought about by political uncertainty in Cuba. Castro's social welfare programs and his assault upon the Cuban economy led to charges, in and outside of Cuba, that he was becoming a communist—a charge he consistently denied.

In a public speech on July 5, 1959, Castro again demonstrated his penchant to control those around him. He demanded that all Cubans support the Revolution, but proclaimed that its leadership must remain in the hands of the small group of revolutionaries. Otherwise, Castro concluded, the Revolution would disintegrate. In short, criticism would not be tolerated. Castro may also have been forewarning the Cubans of what soon followed.

Castro's decrees, policies, and brutal justice were not without opposition. Within Cuba, it came from wealthy landowners, U.S. business interests, and those with ambition who had supported the Revolution, but now were denied a share of the power. And Castro's decision to run the government the only way he knew how, to control it himself, led critics to accuse him of being intoxicated with power.

The Revolution came under attack from former Cuban politicians who not only criticized the Agrarian Reform Law and Urban Reform Law, but also Castro's failure to hold the elections he had promised. There also was dissension within Castro's ranks. For example, in late June 1959, the commander of the Air Force, Pedro Díaz Lanz, resigned his position and defected to the United States, where he denounced Castro's drift toward communism. Denying reality, Castro charged that the criticism came from former Batista supporters. To strangle the critics and the opposition, Castro engineered the amending of the 1940 constitution to allow the death penalty for counterrevolutionary activities. Castro used this authority to send yet another signal to the Revolution's opponents. Selective arrests of conservative political opposition leaders immediately followed.

Within Castro's administration, President Urrutia had become a liability for not being in step with the young revolutionaries. When he attempted to drive a wedge between Castro and the Communists, Castro reacted. In a carefully orchestrated manner, Castro announced his resignation on the morning of July 17 and then denounced Urrutia on national television that evening. Castro attacked Urrutia's wealth and lifestyle and charged that he was linked to factions in the United States determined to intervene in Cuba so that the United States could again dominate Cuba's internal affairs. Without a real power base of his own, Urrutia resigned, and was replaced by Osvaldo Dorticós, a successful lawyer from the middle class currently serving as minister of revolutionary laws. The denunciation of Urrutia was part of a larger plot that Castro revealed on July 26, the sixth anniversary of the Moncada raid and a national holiday. A huge crowd gathered in the Civic Plaza. Many were peasants trucked in from the countryside. To the cheering crowd, and as planned, President Dorticós announced that, in response to overwhelming public demand, Castro would resume his role as prime minister. In a fashion to be repeated several times over the next 50 years, Castro strengthened his hand over government control.

Outside of Havana a major center of opposition rested in Camagüey Province. Conservative cattle ranchers strongly objected to the Agrarian Reform Law and there was demonstrative public protest over the increasing communist influence in government. It was in Camagüey that Raúl Castro and Che Guevara had been indoctrinating local troops and government employees with communist ideology. The protests came not only from anticommunists, but also from loyal supporters of Fidel who, they assumed, in light of his public disavowals of communism, must not have been aware of what his brother was doing.

Fidel squashed the protest in dramatic fashion. In October 1959, Hubert Matos, military commander of Camagüey and a loyal veteran of the Sierra Maestra campaign, decided to resign, a step he hoped would force Fidel to become aware of the growing Communist influence in the military. Instead, Matos was denounced as a traitor to the Revolution, ostensibly on the basis of his sympathy with those who opposed agrarian reform in Camagüey Province. Fidel arrived in the city of Camagüey and ordered the arrest of Matos and 20 other officers who resigned with him. Fidel then appointed Camilo Cienfuegos to succeed Matos and his brother Raúl as Minister of the Armed Forces, a position that gave him cabinet rank. Fidel's action sent a signal to both the political left and right. It meant that Fidel condoned his brother's actions. By making an example of Matos a forceful signal was sent to the right. More important, the entire affair demonstrated Castro's intolerance of any dissidence, no matter how close a supporter. As a result of the Matos affair, Castro further consolidated his political power.

The Matos affair had wider implications. In January 1959, Castro gathered around him a number of brilliant young economists, including the Director of the National Bank, Felipe Pazos, and in the Ministry of Finance, Rufo López Frequet, Ernesto Betancourt, Faustino Pérez, and, Manuel Ray. By July 1959, this group became disillusioned with Castro's ideas, most of which lacked a sound economic basis. When Castro went after Hubert Matos, in the fall of 1959, Pazos resigned as Bank Director. Subsequently, the other well-trained economists departed government and Cuba. Pazos was replaced by Che Guevara, whose lack of economic training and Marxist leanings were well known. Che Guevara was not the only known Marxist to gain prominence in government circles.

Despite their long-standing mutual mistrust, Castro and Cuba's communist PSP became strange bedfellows. Recognizing the party's influence over labor, Castro permitted communists to assume leadership roles in the organization of labor. And understanding that many PSP members were well educated and trained, Castro assigned them to positions in the government bureaucracy. For many longtime communists, like Blas Roca and Raúl Roa, who adhered to Moscow's line, the opportunity to participate in shaping the Revolution could not be denied. These actions became a self-fulfilling prophecy. As communists replaced noncommunists, more of the latter departed government service and the country.

Urrutia, Díaz Lanz, and Pazos were among the most notable persons frustrated at the direction Cuba was now taking under Castro's leadership. They joined others who departed before them and thousands of others would soon follow. On January 1, 1959, the day Batista departed from Cuba, an estimated 500 of his closest supporters fled to the United States. By the end of June 1959, 26,000 more followed. A second wave of 83,500 Cuban immigrants came to the United States during 1960 and by the time of the Cuban Missile Crisis in October 1962, nearly 250,000 Cuban exiles arrived stateside. They joined an estimated 125,000 Cuban Americans and their descendents who had been migrating to the United States since the nineteenth century. Among those who deserted Castro's cause were Teresa Casuso and Eloy Gutiérrez-Menoyo. Casuso, who had assisted Castro during his exile in Mexico, declared herself to be the ambassador of the revolutionary government to Mexico in 1959, and shared the 1960 New Year's Eve with Fidel and his supporters, became disappointed with Castro in 1960. She could no longer support the Revolution. Its dream of a democratic Cuba had been lost. Gutiérrez-Menoyo, one of many students who called for the downfall of the Batista regime starting in 1952, later formed his own military brigade to join in the battles of the Sierra Maestra. In fact, his army surpassed in size that of Fidel Castro's and it was the first to arrive in Havana. Gutiérrez-Menoyo actually handed Havana over to the 26th of July Movement on January 1, 1959, but he became increasingly disillusioned and departed for Miami in January 1961, where he founded Alpha 66 to conduct clandestine raids upon Cuba. From another base in the Dominican Republic, he launched an attack upon Cuba in December 1964, only to be caught and sentenced to 30 years in prison.

The first wave of Cuban arrivals to the United States in 1959 came largely from the upper class that had been closely associated with the Batista regime. The second wave represented the middle class—government technicians, medical personnel, professionals, and managers of the nationalized industries. Stripped of their wealth before departing, these embittered Cubans sought quick revenge against Castro. Many of them organized into paramilitary groups—Omega 7 and Alpha 66, for example—in southern Florida from where they conducted commando raids against the Cuban coastal cities.

The Eisenhower administration welcomed these Cuban émigrés on humanitarian grounds and used their plight to reaffirm the public image that Castro was drifting toward communism. The administration also understood that the loss of the talented upper and middle sectors would have an adverse impact upon the Cuban economy.

In addition to his increased control over government and society and the leftward drift of his regime, Castro's early foreign policy bolstered his image as a revolutionary bent on taking advantage of Latin America's socioeconomic and political ills. At the time of Castro's Revolution, most Latin American governments were controlled by military generals or by landed elites propped by the military. In addition, a widening income gap and the concomitant social consequences presented an enormous challenge to existing governments and potential opportunities for would-be revolutionaries, like Fidel Castro. In 1958, Brazilian President Juscelino Kubitschek convinced U.S. Treasury Secretary, C. Douglas Dillon, of the danger caused by political dictatorship and socioeconomic disparities. In response, the Eisenhower administration established the Social Progress

Trust Fund, a forerunner to the Alliance for Progress, by which the United States sought to address Latin America's socioeconomic ills and bring about political reform. A 1959 joint U.S. congressional inquiry into Latin America concluded that it was just these conditions that Castro had capitalized upon in Cuba.

Castro understood the same and, in fact, often pondered the possibilities of hemispheric uprisings against the established order. As time passed, he even encouraged such movements, but apparently not in 1959. Three events that year sent mixed signals. In April, while Castro visited the United States, a group of 84 Panamanians and Cubans departed the island for the isthmian republic, but were intercepted by Panamanian authorities before landing. Three Panamanians and two Cubans were taken to Panama City. When Fidel learned of the event, he chastised his brother Raúl. Although no record of the conversation exists, Fidel's subsequent public criticism of unidentified Cuban officials for permitting the rebels to use Cuba as a base and then not prevent their departure, led to the conclusion that Fidel played no role in the affair. In June, a group of Nicaraguans launched an unsuccessful invasion of Nicaragua from Costa Rica to oust Luis Somoza. Its failure led to the disbandment of another Nicaraguan exile group then training in Cuba.

The Dominican Republic was another story. Its sugar-based economy, controlled by the elite and protected by dictator General Rafael Trujillo, mirrored the Cuban experience. Castro envisioned the Dominican's departure since his participation in an aborted attempt in 1947. More recently, it was Trujillo who provided safe haven for Fulgencio Batista before he moved on to Spain. Thus, in post-1959, Castro permitted Dominican exiles to plot and to train in Cuba in anticipation of returning home. In June 1959, Delio Gómez Ochoa led 200 Dominicans and 10 Cubans ashore on the Dominican Republic's northern coast. The invasion, reminiscent of Castro's landing at Santiago de Cuba in December 1956, ended before any of the rebels could escape into the countryside. In the aftermath, Castro could not escape the international criticism he received for harboring the rebels.

As Castro maneuvered for power after January 1959, he continued his affairs with other women, but in the end one, Cecilia Sánchez, emerged as his closest confidante. In February 1959, Fidel commenced a four-month relationship with Marita Lorenz, the 19-year-old daughter of a German ship captain, whose *Berlin* visited Havana that month. Reportedly, he had another affair with an attractive Argentinian woman, Dr. Lidia Vexel-Robertson, whom Castro met during his trip to New York. But it was Cecilia Sánchez who emerged at the center of Castro's life. Born to a physician in Oriente Province, Cecilia sent supplies and food to Castro and his colleagues during their imprisonment on the Isle of Pines. When Castro took to the Sierra Maestra in December 1956, she organized supply lines to the rebel group and subsequently joined the rebel forces. On May 28, 1957, in the battle at Uvero, Cecilia became the first woman combatant in the revolutionary army and later formed the Mariana Granjales Platoon. When Castro arrived in Havana on January 8, 1959, Cecilia was not far behind, but she was not pleased with Fidel's dalliances, particularly with Vexel-Robertson. Reportedly, Cecilia made threats to both Fidel and Vexel-Robertson. Eventually, Vexel-Robertson married another rebel and returned to the United States. Whatever the truth, by late 1959 Sánchez became Fidel's private secretary. Eventually she would serve on the Communist Party Central Committee.

It was not Castro's personal life, but his domestic and foreign policies that became the focus of U.S. policy. Castro's crackdown on opposition at home, his association with other rebel groups, real or imagined, and his continued attacks upon the United States caused the Eisenhower administration, in November 1959, to conclude that there was no reasonable basis to believe that Castro would adopt policies consistent with U.S. security or economic interests. In the larger hemispheric policy considerations, the Eisenhower administration confronted the reality that Castro-type revolutions, caused by disparate socioeconomic conditions and political dictatorships, were a possibility. Castro's confrontation with the United States reached a climax in 1960. Castro's actions further convinced the Eisenhower administration that, indeed, Castro was a communist.

Castro's early economic policies and generous spending habits may have satisfied Cuban nationalism, but they effectively squandered away the financial reserves inherited from the Batista regime and prompted him to search for new trading partners. In October 1959, at the INRA headquarters, Castro met with Alexander Alekseyev, a KGB agent in Cuba disguised as a journalist for *Tass*. Castro talked about trade, and Alekseyev talked about restoring diplomatic relations, which Batista had severed in 1952. As a result of this meeting, the Soviets agreed to send to Cuba their trade fair exhibition, currently in New York City and scheduled to visit other Latin American countries, accompanied by First Deputy Premier, Anastas Mikoyan. Fidel Castro could not have been happier on February 4, 1960, when Mikoyan and his group arrived at Havana's José Martí International Airport. Castro also had to be pleased with Mikoyan's public address that extolled the virtues and successes of the Soviet Union's planned economy. A managed economy, Mikoyan asserted, brought the benefits to all the people, whereas in the capitalist system the owners enjoyed success at the expense of the workers. The agreements reached during Mikoyan's visit tied the Cuban economy closer to that of the Soviet Union and opened the door to the Eastern European bloc countries. The Cubans received a 12-year credit of $100 million at 2.5 percent interest for the purchase of Soviet commodities, and Soviet technical assistance for the construction of plants and factories. The Soviets also agreed to purchase five million tons of Cuban sugar over the next five years. The agreements contained some downsides—the Soviets would pay about half of what the Cubans received from the United States for sugar, and the Soviets charged the Cubans more for their oil than other consumers. As expected, Eastern European bloc countries followed the Soviets to Cuba. The East Germans came first. Poland, Romania, and Bulgaria soon followed, each signing a barter agreement to receive Cuban agricultural products in exchange for manufactured goods. And when the fair closed, the Soviets left behind the majority of the machinery, including a modern helicopter for INRA, which Castro quickly appropriated for his own use.

During the three-week visit, the trade fair attracted about one million Cuban visitors, but not everyone was as impressed as Castro. From the start, student dissidents disrupted Mikoyan when he spoke publicly. *Bohemia* ran stories and printed photographs depicting the shoddiness of Soviet housing, equipment, and consumer goods, and made a special point of the rubble left behind in Budapest by the Soviet army in 1956 when it suppressed an autonomous movement in that country. Longtime Castro friend Luis Conte Agüero repeated *Bohemia's* attack upon the Soviet Union during his popular television program. Significance is given to the criticisms leveled by Agüero and Angel Quevedo, editor of *Bohemia*, because each had been longtime supporters of Fidel but saw he and his Revolution drifting toward communism. So too, did the United States, which charged that the agreements violated the Monroe Doctrine that, since 1823, declared the Western Hemisphere was off limits to foreign interlopers. The governments in Havana and Moscow scoffed at the U.S. assertion.

Mikoyan's visit and the resultant trade agreement led to the restoration of diplomatic relations between Cuba and the Soviet Union. The Soviets did not share Castro's belief that the restoration of diplomatic relations would not only accelerate economic relations, but also serve as an insurance policy against any U.S. aggression directed toward Cuba. At the moment, Moscow policymakers were unsure of Castro's intentions or of his political survival. Instead, the Soviets placed the relationship within the larger context of their Latin American policy at the time—exploit economic opportunities as they presented themselves. Still, the Soviet connection emboldened Castro to take steps that drew countermeasures from the United States ending with the severance of diplomatic relations in January 1961.

On March 4, 1960, a month after Mikoyan's visit, the French ship *La Coubre* exploded in Havana harbor. Included in its general cargo were Belgian-made small arms and ammunition. Despite all evidence to the contrary, Castro placed blame upon the United States and used the incident to further stir the anti-American sentiment on the island. Comparing the incident to the 1898 *Maine* disaster, Castro implied that only the Americans could be responsible for the explosion. The incident served notice that, henceforth, every incident or policy failure within Cuba was caused by the United States.

In the early spring of 1960, Castro needed to confirm his control over Cuba and to obtain badly needed foreign assistance. With the link to the United States in jeopardy, the Soviet Union appeared as a viable option. But Castro needed to attract Moscow's attention. To do so, Castro used the 1960 May Day (May 1) celebrations to declare Cuba a Socialist state. Fidel also announced that there would not be elections every four years, as provided in the 1940 Constitution, because the Revolution was a direct expression of the people. Henceforth, the people voted everyday by their support of the Revolution. Critics correctly noted that Castro feared elections might eject him from power. More important at the time was to lure the Soviets to the Caribbean.

Following Castro's May Day declaration, the pace of confrontation with the United States accelerated. On May 23, 1960, Castro ordered Standard Oil, Texaco, and Royal Dutch Shell to refine six thousand barrels of Soviet crude oil daily. The companies were willing to do so, but the U.S. State Department directed them to do otherwise, believing it would lead to a crippling of the Cuban economy. Castro responded by nationalizing the refineries. Castro's action strengthened the opinion of U.S. policymakers that Castro was, indeed, a communist.

The increasing anti-American character of Fidel Castro's regime in Cuba provoked the U.S. Congress to drastically cut the Cuban sugar quota in legislation it approved on July 3, 1960. The measure evolved from debates regarding the extension of the 1948 Sugar Act that had established quotas for domestic and foreign producers of sugar and provided for a uniform price of about two cents per pound above those in the world market. Under this law and its extensions in 1952 and 1956, Cuba provided the United States with about one-third of its sugar needs. In 1960, the introduction of a Democratic Party proposal to increase the amount of Cuban sugar imports touched off a bitter congressional debate regarding U.S. support of the Castro regime. The debate included a proposal to extend the Sugar Act for one year and, at the same time, authorize the president to cut Cuba's quota. On June 30, the House of Representatives unanimously approved a measure to extend the Sugar Act for one year, until December 31, 1961, to grant the president the authority to cut the Cuban quota for 1960 and 1961, and to assign any Cuban losses to other foreign producers. In deference to domestic sugar growers, the Senate version did not contain the latter proviso. Finally, in an all-night session, July 2–3, a House-Senate conference committee approved the final measure that provided the president with authority to cut Cuban sugar imports.

President Eisenhower promptly signed the legislation into law and with equal haste implemented it. On July 6 he ordered a 700,000-ton cut in Cuba's 3,119,656-ton 1960 quota. Because 2,379,203 tons had already been shipped or certified for shipment, Eisenhower's action effectively reduced the U.S. import of Cuban sugar to 39,752 tons for the remainder of 1960.

Rather than buckle to U.S. economic pressure, Castro immediately decreed the Law of Nationalization that authorized the expropriation of American properties at the discretion of the Cuban executive. Castro felt more secure on July 10, when Soviet Premier Nikita Khrushchev announced that the Soviet Union would purchase the 700,000-ton shortfall for 1960 and announced that figuratively speaking he would use Soviet rockets to defend the Cuban people against U.S. aggression. Khrushchev again taunted Eisenhower with the assertion that the Monroe Doctrine was a policy of the past and that he could not keep communism out of the Western Hemisphere. Although Castro publicly applauded Khrushchev's speech as a Soviet commitment to defend the Cuban Revolution from a U.S. attack, privately, Castro fretted. He was not pleased with the Soviet rocket rattling on his behalf. Privately, Castro saw it as another attempt to insult and threaten the independence of his country.

Conventional wisdom suggests that Castro allied himself with the Soviet Union because he needed their protection and economic assistance. It should be remembered that it was the Soviets who came to the Cubans. In the late 1950s, the Soviet Union gained a new sense of confidence as a result of its economic recovery following Word War II, its apparent control over Eastern Europe, and an end to the Stalin period. With these successes, the Soviets acquired the capability and willingness to underwrite a revolution 8,000 miles from its border.

For Castro, the Soviet connection encouraged him to behave like a nineteenth-century Latin American caudillo—one who ruled without question according to their own personal power and interests.

Emboldened by the professions of Soviet support, the Cuban government seized 37 U.S.-owned sugar mills, valued at $260 million according to the Cuban government. Among the U.S. properties seized were the Cuban Portland Cement Company, Owens Illinois Glass Company, Swift and Company, Armour and Company, and the Moa Bay nickel and cobalt plant. By November 1960, the U.S. Commerce Department reported that more than $1 billion in direct U.S. investments in Cuba had been taken over by the Cuban government. Compensation was to be paid on the basis of Cuban government valuations from a fund created by the proceeds of sales of sugar to the United States in excess of 3.5 million tons at a price of at least 5.75 cents per pound. The landowners were to receive 30-year bonds bearing 2 percent interest with service contingent upon the aforementioned fund. Because the fund would have no resources until U.S. purchases of Cuban sugar reached amounts not attained since World War II, and at prices well above those prevailing in the world market at that time, it was clear that the law's intent was the confiscation of U.S. properties without compensation.

The nationalization process was not restricted to foreign properties. In the course of 1960 all major firms in Cuba were nationalized including, textiles, tobacco, cement, banks, and department stores.

Convinced of a communist threat to the hemisphere, the Eisenhower administration took the issue to the OAS. At the Seventh Meeting of the Ministers of Foreign Affairs in San José, Costa Rica, in August 1960, the United States won approval of a declaration that, although it did not specify Cuba, condemned intervention or threat of intervention by any extra-continental power, and that such a threat endangered the security of the Americas. Unmoved by the Declaration and buoyed by Khrushchev's braggadocio, Castro forecast the overthrow of Latin American governments that signed the San José Declaration.

Castro also took to the international arena, and his decisions that followed gave further evidence to the Eisenhower administration's belief that the Cuban was indeed, a communist. During the San José Conference, Cuba reached a trade agreement with Communist China, whereby the latter agreed to purchase 500,000 tons of Cuban sugar over the next 5 years. In return, Cuba extended recognition to the government at Beijing and severed its ties with Nationalist China. Next, Castro addressed the United Nations General Assembly for four and one-half hours on September 26, 1960. He again criticized the past U.S. presence in Cuba and described its current acts as "economic aggression." As the fall of 1960 progressed, the Cuban government continued its expropriation of U.S.-owned properties.

If cutting Cuba's sugar quota was not enough to curtail Castro's actions, the U.S. administration decided to go further. On October 19, Eisenhower embargoed all trade with Cuba, except for food and medicine, and on the next day, October 20, U.S. Ambassador Philip W. Bonsal was recalled from Havana. To strengthen the embargo, the State Department directed U.S. citizens not to travel to Cuba, except for compelling reasons; nations receiving U.S. aid were advised not to purchase Cuban sugar with U.S. funds; and efforts were made to deny Cuba credit to import spare parts from the United States or its allies. The U.S. Senate also voted to cut mutual security appropriations to any country supplying Castro with military or economic assistance.

From there, U.S.-Cuban relations spiraled downward until January 2, 1961, when Fidel Castro charged that the U.S. embassy in Havana was a center for counterrevolutionary activities and demanded that the embassy staff be reduced to 11 persons within 48 hours. Eisenhower felt he had no choice but to sever diplomatic relations. Eisenhower left the presidency with the Cuban situation most volatile. Economic sanctions failed to force Castro from his leftist direction, leaving the CIA covert operation plan as the only option awaiting incoming President John F. Kennedy. According to the CIA plan, which Eisenhower approved in March 1960, Cuban exiles had been training in Guatemala and Nicaragua for a return to the island, which the CIA predicted would ignite a popular uprising that would topple Castro.

President-elect John F. Kennedy learned of the CIA plan in late November 1960 during a briefing from the Agency's Director, Allen Dulles. In discussions with Kennedy on December 6, 1960, and January 11, 1961; outgoing President Eisenhower encouraged the acceleration of the plan's implementation. Like Eisenhower, Kennedy came to office believing that Castro had undermined the ideals of the Revolution. As another "Cold Warrior," Kennedy viewed Castro as a communist and, as such, determined that Castro had to be removed from power. Whatever the plan to accomplish that objective, Kennedy concluded that the United States should be distanced from it.

After taking office, on January 28, 1961, Kennedy directed the Pentagon to assess the planned invasion and the State Department to assess the political consequences of the proposed operation. On March 19, the Joint Chiefs of Staff's (JCS) evaluation of the plan, which included an on-site visit to the Cuban exiles training base in Guatemala, was submitted to the State Department. The JCS concluded that the plan could be carried out with the required secrecy, but that its ultimate success depended upon the anticipated internal uprising in Cuba. The State Department was less enthusiastic, concerned over the possible political fallout in Latin America and with the United Nations. The State Department preferred the diplomatic and economic isolation of Cuba. Presidential advisor Arthur Schlesinger, Jr., cautioned that the Cuban exiles could not remain in Guatemala indefinitely and that the United States might be rushed into a course of action because the CIA had no other plans for the Cuban brigade, except to bring them back to the United States where their presence would be a political embarrassment. Finally, domestic considerations influenced Kennedy's decision. At home, he faced charges of being soft on communism. At a National Security Council meeting on March 11, 1961, Kennedy directed the CIA to devise a plan to transport the Cuban brigade to the island and for the State Department to prepare a White Paper on Cuba and a presentation to the OAS. Kennedy decided to eject Castro from power.

With apparent hesitancy, the Kennedy administration moved toward the implementation of the invasion plan. While the CIA proceeded with the selection of possible landing sites in Cuba, other civilian advisors cautioned the president in White House meetings on April 4 and 11, 1961. In addition to Schlesinger, Chester Bowles and J. William Fulbright forewarned of the adverse impact that such an invasion would have upon U.S. relations with Latin America; such an invasion contravened the OAS charter and it was doubtful that the U.S. role in the affair could be kept secret. Kennedy approved the operation on the assumption that U.S. support would remain covert. He made it clear that U.S. troops would not be committed if the invasion ran into trouble.

The brigade departed Puerto Cabezas, Nicaragua, on April 12 and landed on April 17 at Playa de Girón (Bay of Pigs). The invasion quickly became a complete debacle. Within two days, and without additional supplies or air cover, the rebel forces crumbled before Castro's army. Some 1,200 men were captured and another 114 exiles died in battle. The anticipated internal uprising never occurred. The captured exiles languished in Cuban prisons until December 1962 when they were released from Cuba in exchange for $35 million in U.S. food, medicine, and medical supplies. They returned to the United States and, at their disembarkation in Miami, Florida, received a hero's welcome. It was a harbinger of the exile community's continued determination to remove Castro from power in Cuba.

At the time, several reasons were given for the invasion's failure. Castro had long anticipated some kind of attack. U.S. news media and Castro's agents, who penetrated the Cuban exile community in Miami, reported on the exiles training in Guatemala. In the days just prior to the invasion, Castro directed the rounding up and detention of all known opponents in Cuba that had been identified by the Committees for the Defense of the Revolution (CDRs). On the military side, a diversionary landing, scheduled for April 14 and 15, to distract from the main invasion, was aborted. Also, Kennedy delayed a second bomb run over Cuba to eliminate Castro's air force. When that attack finally came on April 18, Cuba's shore batteries shot down the three B-26 aircraft sent on the mission. The batteries also destroyed two supply ships waiting offshore.

Clearly, the U.S. government failed to recognize the magnitude of the operation required to overthrow the Fidel Castro regime and to make the necessary commitment of resources, including U.S. troops. The U.S. planners also took at face value the Cuban exile community's assertion that there was massive discontent with Castro among all of Cuba's social sectors. This was not the case. The exile community represented Cuba's middle and upper sectors and, as in their past, misunderstood the lower socioeconomic groups.

Within a week of the disaster, Kennedy appointed an ad hoc committee to investigate the affair. Named after its chairman General Maxwell Taylor, the Taylor Commission's full report did not become public until April 2000. Its most significant disclosure revealed that on April 9, 1961, the CIA learned that the Soviet Union knew the exact details of the plan, including time and place and presumably passed this information on to Castro, key to his controlling potential dissidents prior to the attack and being able to better prepare for it.

In the aftermath of the failed attack, Kennedy was rebuked by critics at home and abroad for interfering in Cuba's internal affairs, leaving the distinct global impression that the United States had not reformed its ways from the early twentieth century and that the Good Neighbor Policy had passed into the night. For Castro, the Bay of Pigs was a success. It strengthened his hand in Cuba. Pictures of him directing military activities at the Bay of Pigs enhanced his popularity and enabled him to consolidate his political base.

Castro also used the prisoners to enhance his image. With the prisoners assembled in the Havana Sports Stadium, on national television Castro spent four hours each of four consecutive days interviewing, debating, and harassing them as he milled among them with a microphone. He debated issues of ideology, politics, history, and racial discrimination. He reminded one prisoner that nowhere else in the world would a prisoner have the privilege to publicly debate with a head of state. Overall, Castro impressed the audience with his audacity, knowledge, and shrewdness. A master manipulator, one could not escape the fact that Castro was in control. Castro used this as a platform to decry Cuba's past exploitation and corrupt governments and the virtues of the Revolution.

The embarrassment caused by the Bay of Pigs fiasco, however, did not deter Kennedy from continuing to seek Castro's removal from power. He pursued a three-pronged policy toward that objective: (1) an economic embargo; (2) the political isolation of Cuba; and (3) the sabotage of the Cuban economy.

By the time of the Bay of Pigs invasion on April 17, 1961, the U.S. national mood was decidedly anti-Castro, with few exceptions. This mood made it easy for Kennedy to impose restrictions on Americans traveling to Cuba, and for congress to abolish the entire Cuban sugar quota on March 31 and to approve legislation on September 4 that imposed a total ban on U.S.-Cuban trade. The Kennedy administration further tightened the economic noose in July 1963, when the Treasury Department banned all financial and currency transactions with Cuba under authority of the Trading with the Enemy Act. Immediately, $33 million in Cuban public and private deposits in the United States were frozen, denying the Cuban government funds to finance revolutions across Latin America, to contract trade with Western Europe, and to use other currencies of less value. Following the congressional imposition of a total embargo, Kennedy sought Canadian and Mexican cooperation in preventing the transshipment of U.S. goods to Cuba. The former proved more cooperative than the latter, but each continued their own trade with Cuba. In 1962, the Kennedy administration aggressively attempted to persuade its West European allies to curtail their shipping to Cuba and the Japanese to find other sources of sugar. The effort proved largely successful, as Cuba's international trade declined by 60 percent from 1962 to 1963. Concerned about straining relations with its allies, the Kennedy administration did not push the matter further before his death in November 1963.

Kennedy moved to isolate Cuba from the Western Hemisphere at the OAS Foreign Ministers meeting in Punta del Este, Uruguay, in January 1962. With Argentina, Brazil, Chile, Ecuador, and Mexico abstaining, the Ministers approved, by the minimum two-thirds majority, a statement declaring that the principles of Marxism-Leninism were incompatible with the principles of the Western Hemisphere and that Cuba be excluded from participation in the inter-American system. Kennedy's successor, Lyndon B. Johnson, completed Cuba's hemispheric isolation. The U.S. embargo was expanded to include all Western Hemispheric nations at the OAS Foreign Ministers meeting in Washington, D.C., in July 1964. By a 15 to 4 margin (Bolivia, Chile, Mexico, and Uruguay voted against the sanctions; Venezuela abstained), the Foreign Ministers approved mandatory economic sanctions on Cuba. The sanctions barred all OAS members from maintaining diplomatic and consular relations with Cuba and required that they suspend all trade with Cuba (except for food and medicines needed for humanitarian reasons) and suspend all sea transportation to Cuba.

In August 1961, Kennedy approved the CIA's plan, dubbed "Operation Mongoose," to sabotage the Cuban economy in hopes that it would lead to an internal uprising that would result in Castro's ouster. A command post was established at Miami, Florida, radio station JM-WAVE to serve as the nerve center of worldwide anti-Castro operations. At its peak, the station had a $50 million operating budget, a permanent staff of more than 300 Americans, and an estimated 2,000 intelligence agents around the globe conducting anti-Castro activities.

At the same time Kennedy was approving the CIA plot, Che Guevara met privately with presidential advisor Richard Goodwin in Punta del Este, Uruguay, in August 1961 where representatives of the Western Hemispheric nations were discussing the Alliance for Progress. Che suggested that the two countries sign an anti-hijacking agreement, with the clear implication that this would be a step toward broader discussions. Goodwin left Uruguay believing that this could be an opening, but the administration had no interest in pursuing the matter. Kennedy was determined to rid Cuba of Castro.

Sabotage teams began infiltrating Cuba in 1962 to destroy strategic projects such as sugar mills, oil refineries, power plants, bridges, communication networks, and the cable car system transporting copper ore from the Matahambre mines. The plan also included attacks upon Cuba's food supplies through crop destruction and shipping containers. The CIA also acted outside of Cuba with the contamination of a cargo of Cuban sugar on a British freighter docked in Puerto Rico and the sinking in the Thames River of a British ship carrying Leyland buses en route to Cuba. Into early 1964 the CIA reportedly sent 50 agents per week into Cuba to carry out the attacks. Thirteen sabotage attacks were carried out between November 1963 and January 1964 alone.

Presidential advisors consistently questioned the effectiveness of the operation, as it enhanced, not destroyed Castro's image at home. Castro astutely used the link between the CIA and the Miami exile community, which carried out the sabotage, to fuel Cuban nationalism. These operations continued until April 1964 when President Lyndon B. Johnson accepted his advisor's recommendations and ordered an end to the sabotage. The official disconnect between the government and the exile community did not prevent the latter from continuing operations on their own.

American efforts to assassinate Castro began in the Eisenhower administration and continued through the Johnson years. Again, the CIA was charged with the responsibility of eliminating Castro. In the spring of 1961, Cuban Army Major and CIA agent, Rolando Cubela, was involved in two attempts against Castro's life. In early 1962, the CIA provided underworld figure John Roselli with poison pills, small arms, and explosives to deliver to his Cuban contacts for use in the elimination of Castro. In 1963, two bizarre plans were attempted: (1) placing explosives in the area where Castro usually went skin diving, and (2) providing him with a contaminated suit. In the fall of 1964 the CIA provided Cubela with high-powered rifles, and a year later with scopes and silencers for those rifles. Cubela's failure to act coincided with the time, June 1965, when President Johnson directed the CIA to abandon its assassination plans.

Under attack from the United States, Castro needed more than economic assistance. He needed military security and, at the moment, Castro decided that the Soviets were the only viable option. To persuade them, Castro took a calculated risk on December 1, 1961. While a guest on the Popular University television show Castro calmly declared that "I am a Marxist-Leninist and shall remain a Marxist-Leninist until the day I die." The Soviets understood, if the Americans did not, that Castro was deliberately trying to involve them in the eternal defense of Cuba. The Soviets also understood, if the Americans did not, that Castro's declaration did not put Cuba in the Soviet camp.

In the spring of 1962, Premier Nikita Khrushchev convinced his reluctant military commanders to place intermediate range ballistic missiles in Cuba. Castro interpreted the decision as one to defend his socialist revolution from a U.S. attack. Although Khrushchev often stated that he would defend Cuba against any U.S. attack, geopolitical reasons were more important in reaching his decision. Because of Kennedy's failure with the Bay of Pigs invasion in April 1961 and the president's perceived weakness at their June 1961 Vienna summit conference, Khrushchev was encouraged to take bolder steps. Khrushchev reasoned that missiles in Cuba gave at least a public challenge to the perception of Soviet missile inferiority, that they strengthened the Soviet hand regarding U.S. missiles in Europe, and that they provided the Soviets with a bargaining chip over Berlin. Still, Khrushchev did not trust Castro. Therefore, he directed that once the missiles were operational, their control and use would be a Soviet responsibility.

As the crisis unfolded Kennedy understood the reasons for Khrushchev's action, but he also labored under other pressures. Kennedy's response is placed within the context of the Monroe Doctrine, which in 1823, declared the Western Hemisphere off-limits to European encroachments. A congressional resolution in late September 1962, before the missile crisis,

authorized direct military intervention in Cuba to rid it of communism. It
not only illustrated the contemporary application of the Monroe Doctrine, but also challenged Kennedy to do something about his perceived
weakness in the face of Soviet aggressiveness. In this atmosphere, one
cannot escape the fact that congressional elections were scheduled for
November 1962.

The Cuban exile community first reported the construction of Soviet
missile sites in Cuba in June 1962, but U.S. authorities dismissed the reports given the community's lack of credibility based upon the inaccurate
information provided on the eve of the Bay of Pigs operation. However,
U-2 photographs taken in late August confirmed the exiles' claim. Subsequent U-2 photographs confirmed that the sites would soon be operational; Kennedy needed to act. In a national television address on
October 22, 1962, the president announced quarantine on the introduction of Soviet offensive missiles into Cuba. Irregardless of the vagaries of
international law on such a quarantine and critics assertions that it might
lead to war with the Soviets, Kennedy explained that the Soviet action
violated a basic principle of U.S. policy that dated to the early nineteenth
century—no foreign interlopers were to be permitted on the island.

For 13 days in October 1962 the world stood in suspense and on the
brink of a nuclear disaster. The crisis eased on October 26 when a Soviet
flotilla of missile-carrying ships stopped dead in its tracks shortly after entering the Atlantic Ocean from the Mediterranean Sea. At the same
time, Khrushchev sent two messages to Kennedy. The first offered to remove the missiles from Cuba in return for a U.S. promise to end its quarantine and not to invade the island. The second was more bellicose. It
charged the U.S. with creating the crisis and demanded the removal of its
missiles from Turkey. In the negotiations that followed, Khrushchev
promised to remove the missiles under United Nations supervision in return for a Kennedy promise to remove U.S. missiles from Turkey and, sec-
ondly, not to invade the island.

While Moscow and Washington settled on their own terms, Castro
prepared a plan for United Nations Secretary General, U Thant. In it,
Castro argued that Kennedy's pledge not to invade Cuba was meaningless
unless the president lifted the embargo on Cuba, stopped all subversive
activities emanating from the United States and Puerto Rico, terminated
all violations of Cuban air space and territorial waters by U.S. planes and
craft, and withdrew from the naval base at Guantánamo and returned it to
Cuba. U Thant saw merit in the proposal, thereby adding to Cuba's international prestige. But his subsequent visit to the island was a failure. Castro's message was clear. The U.N. could negotiate on Castro's behalf, but

only if its objectives mirrored those of Castro. No one in the international community could control him. Cuban sovereignty was more important than superpower interests.

As the missile crisis came to its conclusion, Castro became increasingly furious. He had prepared the nation for a war, only to become a pawn between the superpowers. Throughout the crisis, neither the United States nor the Soviet Union consulted with him. In the end, Castro felt abandoned by the Soviets with their decision to dismantle and remove the missiles he thought were sent to defend him against a U.S. attack. Castro was so disappointed with Moscow's behavior, he refused the admission of U.N. inspectors into Cuba to oversee the missiles' dismantling. The United States had to be satisfied with air surveillance.

In a letter to Khrushchev, Castro revealed how dismayed and disappointed he was in the Soviet response to the U.S. challenge. But Castro also understood that he could not jettison the Soviets, nor could he ignite anti-Soviet feeling in Cuba. The Soviet Union remained Cuba's best hope for survival. Khrushchev, although upset at Castro's tirade, had his own problems. Not only did he provide Kennedy with a victory, but he also embarrassed a Soviet ally, Cuba, before the world. Given his plight, Khrushchev took the lead in mending the fences. He ordered the playing of the "Hymn of the Twenty-sixth of July" at the fortieth anniversary parade of the Bolshevik Revolution on November 7, 1962, the first time ever a foreign anthem was played at the event. Despite a frigid cold and inclement weather, key Soviet officials greeted the Cuban trade delegation when it arrived at the Moscow train station that December, and Fidel himself was invited to the Soviet Union.

For 40 days, beginning on April 19, 1963, Castro traveled throughout the western part of the Soviet Union. He stood atop Lenin's tomb in Red Square with Khrushchev and his colleagues and received numerous honors and accolades at his various stops. In turn, Castro mesmerized his audiences, took impromptu strolls among the Russian people, and marveled at the advances in Soviet machinery. Reportedly, he had a dalliance with a Soviet woman while visiting Kiev. The essence of the Soviet-Cuban rapprochement was sugar. In an ironic turn in Cuban history, Khrushchev convinced Castro that Cuba's economic future rested with sugar and that the Soviets would increase their purchase of it at a higher price. The Soviet leader promised the Cuban that within two years, Soviet technology would produce a mechanized cane cutter. Khrushchev's proposals paralleled the Soviet connection with Eastern Europe—weave the Cuban economy into the Soviet sphere so that it could not act independently. For Castro, it would be a return to the past that he despised—now it

would be with the Soviet Union, not the United States. To expect Castro
not to act independently, however, was expecting too much.

In a four-hour television interview upon returning home, Castro attempted to undo the criticisms he laid upon the Soviets over the missile
crisis and Cuba's return to dependency upon sugar. Castro portrayed
Khrushchev as a wise and humane leader who led his nation to economic
greatness and, in the events of October 1962, kept the world from war.
Castro went on to applaud the Russian people and their alleged socioeconomic advances. It was a model to be emulated, he told the Cuban people. As a result of these realities, Castro explained that Cuba could not
become a diversified industrial nation within five years. Not only did it
lack the natural resources and technology, but also the managerial skills
thanks to past U.S. imperialism and the contemporary U.S. embargo. To
return to the prosperity of the past Castro demanded discipline, hard work,
and perseverance from the Cuban people. There could be no slacking.

Ever the pragmatist, Castro also sought rapprochement with the
United States. Under siege from "Operation Mongoose," and desirous for
greater freedom of action vis-à-vis the Soviet Union, Castro made concil-
iatory gestures toward the United States through Carlos Lechuga, Cuba's
Ambassador to the United Nations. President Kennedy accepted the
overture and through his intermediaries, Robert Kennedy and McGeorge
Bundy, suggested that Lechuga and Dr. René Vallejo, Castro's personal
physician, work out a possible agenda. A month later, French journalist
Jean Daniel interviewed President Kennedy, whose signals of conciliation
were passed on to Castro when Daniel met with him in Havana on November 23, 1963, the same day of Kennedy's assassination in Dallas. With
Kennedy's death, efforts at rapprochement would await another day. New
President Lyndon B. Johnson did not pursue the matter and soon became
deeply involved in his own reelection and subsequently with the implementation of the "Great Society" programs and the Vietnam War. Even if
he had wished to, Johnson could not go forward, as U.S. public opinion
grew increasingly hostile toward Castro in the months following
Kennedy's death. There were constant rumors linking Castro to Lee Har-
vey Oswald and the Mafia, both accused of playing a role in the president's
assassination. Castro consistently denied both.

Following the death of his mother on August 6, Castro decided that his
private life would no longer be public knowledge. Henceforth, the Cuban
press said nothing about how he spent his nonworking hours and his relationship with other people. In fact, most of his inner circle didn't know either. The privacy contributed to his charismatic image and, as he would

admit, provided him greater time and freedom to devote to implementing the Revolution.

Cuba's public euphoria that erupted with Castro's arrival in Havana on January 8, 1959, soon evaporated as the revolutionary leader consolidated his political power and silenced his opposition. With Castro's failed economic policies and spendthrift social welfare programs, the public mood became near despondent by 1962. As always, Castro did not place responsibility for Cuba's plight at his own doorstep, but at that of the United States, an action that would be repeated for the next 40 years. He found a new friend in the Soviet Union, but it proved to be a shotgun wedding. Their divergent reasons for coming together created a mutual mistrust that lasted until the collapse of the Soviet Union in 1991.

Above:
Castro: The Revolutionary.
Library of Congress.

Left:
Castro in the Sierra Madre.
Library of Congress.

Castro and the Triumph of the Revolutionary. Reprinted, by permission, from the Library of Congress.

Castro Meets Khrushchev in New York, September 1960. Library of Congress.

Above:
Castro Addresses the Cuban People, July 27, 1998. Reprinted, by permission, from AP/ Wide World Photos.

Right:
Castro: The Elder States- man, November 16, 1996. Reprinted, by permission, from AP/ Wide World Photos.

Chapter 4

THE INSTITUTIONALIZATION
AND STAGNATION OF
CASTRO'S REVOLUTION

In the 35 years following Fidel Castro's declaration that he was a Marxist-Leninist in December 1961, Cuba experienced three distinct phases of development: (1) the 1960s, during which Castro consolidated his power and attempted to diversify the economy; (2) the 1970s, during which Cuba appeared to benefit from economic reforms; and (3) the 1980s, when the Revolution stagnated.

Throughout the 35-year period, the Cuban leadership adjusted to realities of the day, but democratic centralism remained the modus operandi. Fidel Castro remained the driving force toward the implementation of a socialist state, from the top, down. He constantly sought to create a national consciousness that was committed to the Revolution. Clearly, the state used its pervasive power arbitrarily to force conformity and stifle opposition, but Castro's charisma and his ability to stir the masses to his cause could not be discounted. In many respects, Castro appeared as a twentieth-century Latin American caudillo, wielding wide authority with apparent popular support. In international affairs, Castro pursued his own foreign policy despite Cuba's economic dependency upon the Soviet Union. A maverick within the Soviet system, Castro gambled that Moscow could not afford to abandon him in the high stakes game of superpower geopolitics. Castro sought to provide Cuba a place in the international arena and, when pragmatism dictated, he sought rapprochement with the United States.

In the months immediately following Batista's ouster, Castro needed to fulfill two objectives simultaneously: gain control over the country's political apparatus; and implement a socialist revolution accompanied by a popular commitment to it. The first would prove easier than the second.

In January 1959, Castro and his cadre of close advisors remained but one element of the many factions that contributed to Batista's ouster. To eliminate his political rivals Castro silenced all political parties (save the PSP) and established popular tribunals. Set up in neighborhoods, factories, and rural areas, these courts imposed penalties, from incarceration to execution, on enemies of the state. The lack of concern for legal correctness and fairness characterized this revolutionary justice even after the popular tribunals were incorporated into the restructured legal system in 1973. In addition, the government imposed tight restrictions on the media and intellectual community. The CDRs reported on any critical discussion of government policies. As a result, by the early 1970s an estimated 20,000 political prisoners languished in Cuba's squalid prisons. Cubans learned to follow the proper code of revolutionary conduct or suffer the consequences.

Beginning in the winter of 1960, the country's restructuring accelerated. A Central Planning Board was formed to consolidate economic power, as in the Eastern bloc countries. New civilian militias of students, workers, and peasants were organized across the country. A Board of Revolutionary Propaganda was formed, which began to refer to Cuba as the first Free Territory of America. In Castro's dramatic 1960 May Day speech, Cubans and the world heard for the first time what was to become the famous *"Cuba sí, Yanqui no!"* (Cuba yes, Yankee no!).

Initially, Castro needed the old-time PSP leadership to provide administrative skills and linkage to the Soviet Union, but he also needed to eliminate those party members who potentially served as focal points of opposition to the Revolution. Castro's need for communist managers within his system significantly contributed to his December 1, 1961, declaration on national television that "I am a Marxist-Leninist and shall remain a Marxist-Leninist until the day I die." Castro explained that he previously concealed this fact, fearing that it would militate against the success of the Revolution. While he shared many of the idealistic goals of Cuban communists since his university days, Castro was never a member of the local party and, in fact, distanced himself from it. In 1964, Castro explained to *New York Times* reporter Herbert Matthews that his evolution toward communism had been gradual and forced by the realities of the time. Unsure of the young revolutionary, the Soviets made no mention of Castro's December 1961 declaration in *Pravda*, or in their subsequent congratulatory message on the anniversary of the Cuban Revolution in January 1962.

To strengthen his political hand, in 1961 Castro fused the PSP, the DR, and the 26th of July Movement into the Organizaciones Revolucionarias

Integradas (ORI). Each had its own strength. In addition to its links with the Soviet Union, the PSP had a long history of organization and appeal to the masses. The DR represented the University of Havana students, long strident anti-*Batistianos* who played a vital role in the success of the Revolution. The 26th of July Movement, like the DR, was long on revolutionary zeal. Because of his experience, PSP leader Anibal Escalante was put in charge of organizing ORI. Escalante proceeded to assign his old communist friends to the most important posts within the bureaucracy and to purge members of the 26th of July Movement. These actions enraged Castro who always believed that he should be in charge. As became his practice, Castro publicly discredited those who challenged his authority. Escalante fell victim to Castro's wrath. On March 27, 1962, Castro began a public attack upon Escalante, accusing him of errors and sectarianism. Subsequently, Escalante was exiled to Moscow and then moved to Prague, Czechoslovakia. He was allowed to return to Cuba in 1964 to manage a small farm, but he continued his criticism of the Revolution's direction. In 1968, Escalante and his followers were accused of organizing a microfaction conspiring against the government. After a long, and mostly secret trial, Escalante and his colleagues received long prison sentences for allegedly passing secrets to the Soviet Union. The Escalante affair demonstrated the struggle of the old and new communists, the latter representing *Fidelismo*. The latter triumphed.

Castro's castigation of Escalante was the first step toward the elimination of PSP leadership from the Revolution. In 1964, the same year that Escalante returned from Prague, the trial of Marcos Armando Rodríguez began. Rodríguez allegedly revealed the whereabouts of DR students who conducted the 1957 raid upon the Presidential Palace in an attempt to kill Fulgencio Batista. At that time, the DR refused to let him participate in planning the attack, but whether he had acted on his own initiative or on orders from the PSP in betraying the four students killed in the police raid on their apartment remains unclear, even today. After his escape to Mexico City, Rodríguez received support from Joaquín Ordoquí and his wife, both prominent PSP members. Subsequently, they assisted Rodríguez in obtaining a scholarship to study in Czechoslovakia and work in the Cuban embassy in Prague, from where he allegedly worked as a double agent for the CIA. But it was the 1957 Palace attack that inspired Castro to have Rodríguez extradited back to Cuba in 1961. After languishing in jail for three years, Rodríguez was brought to trial. It was a public spectacle in which PSP leaders—Faure Chomón, the Ordoquí's, Edith García Buchea, and Carlos Rafael Rodríguez—were brought before the court to defend themselves against the accusations that they had assisted Rodríguez seven years earlier. On March 23, 1964, Castro himself took over the proceedings, which were telecast nationwide. For four hours he harangued and hassled Rodríguez, charging that he alone was responsible for the deaths of the four students. Castro so mesmerized the 600 spectators in the courtroom, that when he finished at 1:30 A.M., they stood and applauded. As expected, Rodríguez was found guilty and subsequently executed.

The trial served two significant purposes. First, Castro established that he was the Maximum Leader. When he took to the bench on March 23, he admitted that no legal precedent existed for such action, but as the one with power in Cuba, he could do as he pleased. No one challenged him. Second, in attacking Rodríguez, Castro exonerated the other PSP leaders, but they never challenged Castro's decisions again. Despite publicly acknowledging his errors, Joaquín Ordoquí and his wife disappeared from public view, leading to speculation that they had been imprisoned. Faure Chomón took Castro's tongue lashing in quiet and remained on as the dutiful Minister of Transportation. Blas Roca, an old-line communist and editor of Hoy, observed that the trial marked the triumph of the Revolution over all those who deviated from its course.

The elimination of the PSP as a political force enabled Castro to replace the ORI with the Parido Unido de la Revolución Socialista de Cuba (PURS) and, in 1965, to proclaim the new PCC and to convene its first Central Committee meeting. Nearly 60 percent of its members were military men, but for all, loyalty to Castro was the litmus test for appointment. Until the 1970s, the PCC remained small and disorganized, with no clearly defined role and relegated to a secondary position vis-à-vis the armed forces. At first, Fidel Castro saw little need for a well-defined and developed party structure, which may have rivaled or even reduced his presidential capacity.

As a result of his political maneuvering Castro served not only as prime minister and commander in chief of the armed forces, but also as secretary of the PCC and top member of the politburo. His brother Raúl was second in command. The interlocking leadership roles of the Castro brothers remained a characteristic of Cuban life until the end of the twentieth century and beyond. Castro controlled membership in the PCC. One gained party membership and, subsequently, government appointments and military rank, only by invitation and professions of loyalty to Castro and his Revolution. By the end of the 1960s, an estimated 55,000 Cubans, out of a population of nearly eight million, claimed party membership.

After November 1959, the revolutionary government also began to exert its control over the CTC labor unions and brought workers into line with the Revolution's goals. Even before the nationalization programs of

1960, the government pressured the workers to curtail their wage and benefits demands. According to Che Guevara, the goal was to instill a commitment to the greater good at the sacrifice of individual benefits. Toward that end, in 1960, technical advisory councils were established in the nationalized industries. Their objective was to educate workers about the production process and develop long-term goals, not to share in management decisions. These were made at the top. The government achieved its control over the CTC at its November 1961 national congress, where PSP and 26th of July Movement spokespersons engineered their own election to leadership positions, including Lazaro Peña as general secretary. Henceforth, unions would be organized by economic sector, not by occupation or trade. All workers in the same enterprise would belong to the same union. The CTC congress also established the union's goals and objectives: increase production and productivity; save raw materials, combat labor absenteeism, organize volunteer work, safeguard working conditions, prevent accidents, and develop work skills. The imperative of economic planning superceded workers' interests. While historic wage scales remained in force for the moment, year-end bonuses and sick leave were terminated. Strikes were forbidden. Unions took on a new meaning—carrying out the Revolution's objectives as determined by Castro and his advisors.

Committing the workers to national objectives broke with the historic role of Cuba's labor unions, but did not end the conflict between labor and management. Although the newly appointed grievance commissions often settled labor disputes on behalf of workers, the Labor Ministry overruled them. Castro charged that the grievance commissions were on the side of vagrancy and absenteeism. In an effort to foster greater discipline and commitment to the Revolution among the workers, in 1964, work councils replaced the commissions. Still, clashes between workers and managers persisted, but the union and management leaders, dependent upon the state for their jobs, continually ruled on behalf of the Revolution and, in so doing, contributed to the workers' continued dissent.

Castro also moved quickly to incorporate outsiders such as women, into the Revolution. The Federation of Cuban Women (FMC) founded in 1960 sought to liberate women through revolutionary programs, not gender-based activism. The FMC gave many women their first opportunity to have a life outside the home. Women constituted a reservoir of support for the Revolution, and the FMC readily tapped into it. In 1962 over 4,000 delegates, representing 376,000 members, attended the FMC congress. At the time, more than 19,000 women who had been household servants had graduated from special schools and were now otherwise gainfully employed. The FMC's seamstress program trained 7,400 rural women to use the sewing machine and, in turn, they became instructors to another 29,000 peasant women. The FMC also trained 11,000 women in first-aid techniques and organized another 62,000 for volunteer work. By the mid-1960s, the FMC pointed to 800 women labor leaders in the food industry, 900 former household servants working as bank clerks, and another 863 as nurses. In all, a sizeable proportion of the 282,069 working women in 1963 were employed in jobs different from what they had in the 1950s.

Despite these advances, in the mid-1960s the FMC admitted that its workers carried out their tasks in mechanical fashion and that the rank and file was becoming apathetic. The national spirit that rallied the people around the Revolution in 1959, the Literacy campaign of 1960, and the Missile Crisis was dwindling. In part, the top-down institutionalization and the growing economic hardships stymied individualism. The quality of life was becoming stagnant.

To further enhance his position and to gain the support of the masses, Castro implemented popular programs. The 1961 "Campaign against Illiteracy" set the tone. Some 300,000 people were mobilized to provide the estimated one million illiterates with basic reading and writing skills and, in the process, promote national solidarity and a belief in the Revolution and its leaders. Because the revolutionary leaders saw education as a means to raise social consciousness and develop a commitment to the Revolution, the state assumed responsibility for education from kindergarten through the university. Religious and private education was abolished. Throughout the 1960s, the government spent an estimated 275 million pesos on education, four times the pre-1959 levels. As a result, the number of schools and students more than doubled in a decade. Although the education programs expanded Castro's base of support, critics pointed to its ideological content at the sacrifice of critical thinking. Indeed, even a friend of the Revolution Jacobo Timmerman noted in his book observing life in Castro's Cuba, that Cuba's vaunted educational reforms left no room for free thinking and, worse, the country had few books to read.

Castro also turned sports into a revolutionary tool. Although baseball had long been considered Cuba's national pastime, Cubans otherwise did not pursue sporting activities with great vigor. In 1961, the revolutionary government established the Instituto Nacional de Deportes, Educación Física, y Recreación (INDER) and established its headquarters in Sport City, a Havana suburb. INDER was empowered to develop a national sports program that would have positive lifelong effects on the population. To Castro, athletes not only contributed to the nation's health but also taught the valuable lesson of collectively working together and advancing Cuba's international prestige. By 1975, INDER reported that 3.5 million Cubans actively engaged in various sporting activities. By that time, Cuba began to achieve success in the Pan American Games and, subsequently, in the Olympics. Castro found particular pleasure when his athletes and teams captured gold medals in baseball, boxing, and track and field at the expense of the United States.

Intellectual life did not escape revolutionary control. In March 1959, *Revolución*, the former underground newspaper of the 26th of July Movement, became the official government newspaper. Its Monday literary supplement, *Lunes*, which offered a wide range of views, earned a reputation throughout Latin America. In addition to its own publishing house, *Revolución* had a record company and a weekly hour-long television program. Its independence was challenged in June 1961 by the old-line communists and resulted in the government's control of all culture.

In 1961, *Revolución* produced a television documentary *PM* that depicted ordinary Cubans in their everyday activities. The Instituto Cubano del Arte y Industria Cinematográfica (ICAIC), dominated by old-line communists, charged that the documentary lacked creative excellence, but more importantly, portrayed Cubans in a negative light. A debate raged for three Saturday meetings in June 1961 at the National Library. Fidel Castro appeared at the final meeting on June 30. After several artists and writers expressed contradictory opinions about the state of Cuban cultural works, including criticisms of individuals, Castro took the microphone. As he prepared to speak, he removed his pistol from its holder and placed it on the table. The gesture was clear. He was in control. His words "within the Revolution, everything; against the Revolution, nothing," thereafter became the hallmark of Cuban art, literature and other writings, movies, and music. The Revolution had rights, he explained, and its first right was to exist. Those attacking the Revolution would be denied rights. Castro's declaration revealed the leadership's fear of the intelligentsia's free thinking. It could not be trusted. To ensure that their writings and artistic work fit within the Revolution, Castro announced that the Consej. Nacional de Cultura (CNC) would provide appropriate guidelines. In reality, Castro would determine what fit within the Revolution.

Lunes became the first victim. It closed its doors. The long-term impact, however, proved more significant. Henceforth, the ICAIC, under the direction of Vincentina Antuña Tavio, produced films containing only the Revolution's ideological message. Foreign films that conveyed messages contrary to the Revolution's ideals were banned from Cuba.

Next, the state gained control over authors and artists through the Unión Nacional de Escritos y Artistas de Cuba (UNAEC). As employees of the state, Castro informed them that they had to descend from their ivory towers and make money for the state through the Casa de las Américas, the national publication office. Others doing research and writing through the National Library or the Academy of Science came under the same strictures. In effect, Castro controlled intellectual freedom; only the true revolutionary intellectual or artist would be supported. Those whose work did not conform to revolutionary dogma or attempted to protest government strictures, including those whose loyalty to the Revolution was even doubted, found themselves without government support to pursue their work and without access to government social services, food rations, and in the most flagrant cases, their jobs. In 1968, the government further clamped down on the intellectual community, effectively contributing to the stagnation of ideas in the arts and literature. Thereafter, until the national crisis of 1991, the quality of Cuban arts and literature languished. Only then did the government admit to the need for reexamining the loss of freedom of expression in the written and visual arts. It had no choice; by then many of Cuba's artists and writers had found their way into the many dissident groups existing clandestinely under Castro's regime.

Until 1963, the journalistic community continued to express itself within a general context of support of the Revolution, but sometimes it offered interpretations that differed from the official line. Even Carlos Franqui, editor of *Revolución*, carried stories that agitated Fidel. Also, he frequently criticized *Hoy* for carrying stories critical of the government. That changed after Castro returned from Moscow in May 1963 where the state run *Pravda* made a significant impression upon him. As a result, Castro abolished *Revolución* and *Hoy* and, in their place, established *Granma* as Cuba's single daily newspaper under the direction of Jorge Enrique Menéndez. Franqui subsequently left Cuba and became a severe critic of Castro. Menéndez understood that *Granma* was to promote the interests of the Revolution, not provide a forum for differing opinion. Menéndez spoke daily with Cecilia Sánchez, a clear indication of Fidel's personal interest in the paper.

Just as Castro created institutions to serve the Revolution's purpose, he eliminated those that appeared to stand in its way. The Roman Catholic Church was one. A brief honeymoon between the Church and the Revolution existed in early 1959, but it began to unravel with the Agrarian Reform Law in May and the subsequent secularization of education and prohibition of religion in the public schools. These actions resulted in protests and demonstrations by Church leaders and the laity. By 1960 Catholics were linked to counterrevolutionary activities and to those protesting the increased communist influence in government. Beginning in 1961, the churches and schools that appeared as the most vocal critics found themselves under military occupation. In the days following the Bay of Pigs, Castro directed the arrest of priests allegedly linked to the plot. He also expelled most foreign clergy from the island. Following the nationalization of all private schools, hundreds of clergy were deported or chose to leave Cuba. Thereafter, the Church maintained a low profile until the late 1980s.

As Castro directed the regimentation of Cuban life, with its concomitant loss of personal freedoms, he increasingly acted like a patriarch—that he, and only he, knew what was best for the people; that he had their best interests at heart; and that they should trust him. There was a costly downside to Castro's behavior and programs. Consumer goods became increasingly scarce and the quality of life decreased. Coupled with the growing power of the secret police, and with the CDRs increasingly intruding into people's lives, fear and distrust was evident throughout much of society. Because of the primacy of his position, Castro became responsible for all that went wrong.

Beginning in 1961, Castro's overriding consideration was to transform the Cuban economy by expanding nonsugar exports, achieving self-sufficiency in food production, and developing an industrialization plan based upon the import-substitution model, all to be achieved while continuing sufficient sugar production to maintain full employment during the transition. Economic success would make it easier to force conformity through the other social and intellectual institutions. Failure would mean that the populace had reason for protest and political change.

Based upon the assumption that Moscow would not want communism to fail within the U.S. sphere of influence, the Cuban leadership anticipated unlimited economic assistance from the Soviet Union and its East European bloc allies. With this confidence, the Junta Central de Planificación (JUCEPLAN) anticipated economic and annual growth to reach 10–15 percent for the 1962–65 time period.

The strategy to achieve this objective was familiar to the old Cuban elite. Sugar production would be expanded to seven million tons per year and agricultural diversification would lead to greater food self-sufficiency. Additional funds would come from savings generated by the drastic cut in luxury imports and continued aid from the Soviets and East bloc countries. Castro also anticipated finding and exploiting large petroleum reserves. Effectively, Cuba would pursue the import-substitution-industrialization model, producing at home what it had previously imported, mostly from the United States.

The plan quickly failed. By 1962, the program was in disarray. That March, for the first time in Cuban history, food rationing began. Scarcities of all consumer goods multiplied thereafter. The reasons were numerous. The government used the 28 million pesos surplus Batista left behind to provide benefits to the masses, leaving none to meet the needs of economic development. Contrary to expectations, central planning was often improvised and chaotic and did not provide quick solutions to economic problems. Persistent delays and bottlenecks plagued the internal distribution system. Industrialization plans failed to materialize, in part because Cuba lacked the essential natural resources and could not afford to purchase them on the world market. Government income declined as sugar production and world prices for it decreased appreciably. In fact, Cuba's trade deficit climbed to $327 million by 1963, of which $197 million was with the Soviet Union alone. The out migration of professionals and skilled technicians exacerbated the situation, and the Cuban workers who remained appeared unmotivated and unprepared to meet the challenges before them. The U.S. embargo disrupted Cuba's previous primary trade relationship and, in the process, Cuba lost a guaranteed sugar market and the source of badly needed spare parts for its machinery. There was more. The anticipated Soviet bloc assistance did not materialize. Rather than look to the shortcomings of their own idealism and inexperience and the weaknesses of centralized planning, Castro placed responsibility elsewhere, particularly on the doorstep of the U.S. embargo.

The failed economic policies caused a debate among the Revolution's leadership. From the start of the Revolution in 1961, Castro accepted the advice of his close friend Che Guevara, a Marxist idealist, but not an economist. As Minister of Industries, which included sugar, Guevara had implemented a highly centralized planning approach and relied upon moral incentives for the workers to produce for the good of the Revolution. It failed, particularly in the sugar industry—a fact Guevara admitted in a July 1963 speech in Algiers. In the leadership debates that followed, Guevara's idealism lost out to the pragmatists, those who believed in quasi-capitalist methods that provided material rewards for workers. Guevara's decline in importance was first registered on July 3, 1963, when he lost direct tutelage of the sugar industry, which now would have its own ministry. At the same time, President Osvaldo Dorticós replaced Regino Boti at the Ministry of Economy and was also named head of the Central Planning Council. Guevara understood that he had lost the power of economic planning. Emphasis was now placed upon the exportation of all agricultural goods in order to earn the foreign exchange needed for the acquisition of machinery and equipment. Industrial planning shifted to the development of those sectors that utilized Cuban natural resources most efficiently.

As a result of the changes in economic policy and the alignment of Cuba with the Soviet Union in January 1964 during Castro's second visit to Moscow, Guevara had been relatively marginalized from the daily running of the economy. Castro attempted to pacify Guevara by making him head of the Cuban delegation to the United Nations Conference on Trade and Development in Geneva in March 1964 and naming him Cuba's representative to the anniversary of the Russian Revolution in November. By the year's end, Guevara felt isolated and alone, yet he remained true to his commitment not to attack Fidel Castro. The feeling was mutual; Fidel had a special relationship with, and fondness for, Guevara.

Guevara's wanderlust and desire for a new adventure led him away from Cuba and into revolutionary ventures in South America. He turned to Bolivia as the place to initiate a new social revolution. The country's large indigenous population (Inca Indians and their descendents) lived on the margins of the national economy and was not represented in the national government. Just what role Castro had in pushing Guevara toward Bolivia is not clear. Although Cuba provided a training ground and supplies for the mission, there is evidence that Castro attempted to dissuade Guevara from the undertaking.

Guevara departed for Bolivia in the fall of 1966 and began his military actions there in March 1967. In the Bolivian Andes Mountains, however, he never attracted the local Indians to his cause. They did not accept the foreigner, nor did they view the world through the same Marxist lens that Guevara did. The Bolivian military, aided by the CIA, pursued Guevara with a vengeance. Guevara's time finally ran out; he was captured and executed by the Bolivian military in the remote Andes on October 9, 1967.

As for Castro, once Guevara arrived in Bolivia, he failed to provide him with the necessary support for victory, nor did he make any effort to rescue Guevara when the opportunity presented itself in July and August 1967, facts that led Guevara to conclude in his diary that he had been betrayed by the Cuban leader. Castro claimed that the Russians had tied his hands, and that the Bolivian communists, hopelessly split among themselves, refused to cooperate in Guevara's rescue.

In reality, Castro could not afford widening the revolutionary spectrum in Latin America and, if he attempted to do so, U.S. President Lyndon B. Johnson, a hard-line "Cold Warrior" stood as a staunch obstacle, threatening to destroy the Cuban Revolution itself. Castro later used Johnson's threat as the reason for failing to rescue Guevara from Bolivia. But what would he have done with the rescued martyr? On the other hand, Guevara may have expected too much. Whatever the controversy, those closest to Castro observed that, at the time, he was truly saddened by the loss of his companion of a thousand battles, but that he had resigned himself to the inevitable outcome of the Bolivian adventure.

In October 1967, Castro used the occasion of Guevara's death to try to instill a fresh sense of purpose and order into the Cuban Revolution. He publicly extolled the virtues of Che's Marxist idealism and bravery for taking up the cause of Bolivia's downtrodden. It had little impact. Thirty years later, in 1997 when Guevara's remains were exhumed from their place below an isolated Andean airstrip and returned to Cuba for a hero's burial, Castro again applauded the Argentine revolutionary. By this time, however, Guevara had become an icon to many left-leaning people throughout the world. Young people especially admired him. In the United States, T-shirts with an image of Che emblazoned on the front sold briskly at rock concerts and in suburban shopping malls—an ironic turn of capitalism cashing in on an anti-capitalist revolutionary. His ideals for social change and his challenge to the established order overshadowed the bloody side of his revolutionary pursuits. His writings were reprinted, and he became the subject of new and analytical biographies, documentaries, and movies.

Meanwhile, in the mid-1960s, as the gap between Castro and Guevara widened and the latter went off to Bolivia, the Cuban economy continued to falter. By the time of Guevara's death in 1967, the reforms introduced in 1964 began to shows signs of failure due to mismanagement and bureaucratic snafus. Production of sugar, tobacco, vegetables, dairy products, poultry, beef, and pork dropped steadily during that time. Worker absenteeism and low productivity crippled the manufacturing sector. Economic growth rates declined precipitously from 9 percent in 1964, to 1.5 percent in 1965 and to a negative 3.7 percent in 1966.

The economic problems prompted another debate within the government. The debate represented the familiar dilemma of communist regimes: how to reconcile Marxist idealism with a pragmatic economic policy. Before his departure, Che Guevara continued to plead the idealistic strategy. The economy would be fully collectivized and directed by a centralized planning authority. It would require a "new man," a Cuban who would work for moral rewards, such as decorations and public praise, and in the process reflect a new and higher degree of political consciousness. Guevara's leading opponent was Carlos Rafael Rodríguez, an economist and longtime Communist Party member. Rodríguez favored a more measured use of central planning, partial reliance on market mechanisms, and autonomy left to individual enterprises. He argued that state enterprises should account for their expenses and earnings. In short, Rodríguez proposed a more conventional path, relying on material incentives instead of only moral ones.

In 1966 Fidel Castro brought the debate to an end. He endorsed Guervara's idealism. Cuba would make a gigantic collective effort accompanied by moral incentives. Castro immediately increased his own power by taking control of the central planning apparatus. He and his lieutenants plunged into the minutiae of economic management. They expressed an endless optimism that characterized the early days of the Revolution and gave them confidence in the new man, one who would put aside personal gain for the collective good. Rather than pay incentives, increased productivity was acknowledged with badges, medallions, and other awards frequently distributed by Castro himself. Castro hoped that his personal appeal and popularity would be sufficient to overcome the people's natural instinct for personal material gain.

The new economic plan also resulted in the nationalization of the remaining 65,000 small businesses, such as restaurants, repair shops, and retail stores. Castro took a greater interest in the economy and even devised a number of micro plans. He even spoke of a moneyless society.

Accompanying the new revolutionary thrust, but given little attention by the outside world, Castro pursued what can be described only as wacky ideas. For example, he launched a campaign to free Cuba of all weeds. On another occasion, without checking for its suitability, Castro ordered the dispatch of workers to establish a ring of coffee plants around Havana. The soil was incapable of sustaining the plants, causing the dream to wither within a year. But cattle were his most incessant focus. He dreamed of creating a new breed through genetic engineering that would bear his name, thus carrying his name to scientific recognition. He was warned by scientists that his plan to cross a Holstein with the Cebú would not produce such a bovine. One such animal was produced named "White Udder" and, upon her death, Castro had the body stuffed and placed in a museum for future generations to admire.

The combination of economic need and a new moral crusade led Castro to call for the production of a 10-million-ton crop of sugar in 1970. Castro wanted the harvest to end all harvests so that Cuba would have the capital to make future economic development viable and usher in an era of social comforts for everyone. To achieve that goal, Castro ordered the cutting of forests and conversion of traditional agricultural lands in order to plant more cane. Monies pumped into the effort were diverted from the production of foodstuffs and consumer goods. At harvest time, or *zafra,* an estimated 1.2 million workers from all sectors of society joined the 300,000 cane cutters. Castro joined in, as did diplomats assigned to Havana from communist countries, including the Soviet Union. Although a record high 8.5 million tons of sugar were harvested, the failure to reach the stated goal had disastrous effects upon the Cuban economy and psyche. More important was the fact that other economic sectors had been ignored in order to reach the sugar objective. The concomitant loss of foodstuffs and consumer goods meant several more years of sacrifice. The national infrastructure fell into further disrepair as maintenance was ignored during the drive for 10 million tons of sugar. The Cuban people were exhausted, physically and mentally.

To the surprise of almost every observer of Cuban affairs, Castro used the anniversary of the Revolution, July 26, 1970, to admit failure and for the first time in public accept personal responsibility. To a large crowd of Cubans gathered in Havana's Plaza de Revolución, Castro blamed the economic failure upon excessive centralization and bureaucratization of decision making by the PCC and state authorities at the expense of the mass organization and the workers. He even offered to resign. But Castro's confession and resignation offer were not bold moves in 1970 because his political opposition had been eliminated and institutional means to replace him did not exist.

The changes in economic policy that followed Castro's 1970 confession were important. Material incentives replaced moral rewards. Workers were paid according to productivity goals. Those who exceeded the established norms received percentage wage increases and exemplary workers received preferential access to consumer goods such as automobiles, television sets, refrigerators, and washing machines. The government also moved against absenteeism. The 1971 anti-loafing law, subsequently incorporated into the 1976 constitution, required that all men between ages 18 and 60 perform productive labor. Health care, education, and old-age pensions remained free; rents were still fixed at 10 percent of income; and many food items remained rationed. But service fees were restored for the use of telephones, local bus transportation, and sporting events, and day care fees were adjusted according to income. The additional income that productive and favored workers earned generated a new purchasing power that, in turn, created a stimulus for consumer goods. Consumers soon found cameras, phonographs, appliances, bicycles, furniture, clothing, kitchenware, jewelry, cosmetics, and perfumes available, but at higher prices than when rationed.

External pressures also forced Castro to institute economic reforms. Frustrated at the waste of its direct economic assistance, which included balance of payments credits, and subsidies for sugar, petroleum, and nickel (estimated at $12.5 billion for the 1970s), the Soviet Union demanded economic reform. Moscow insisted upon the implementation of the Sistema de Dirección y Projecto Economica (SDPE) that introduced limited market reforms and expanded autonomy for state enterprises, such as the farmers' free markets, where foodstuffs were sold at prices dictated by supply and demand. The government also improved its efficiency. Planning techniques and data collection improved, and a cost accounting system was introduced. The government gave new attention to the training of technicians, economists, systems analysts, and business administrators. In addition, during the 1970s, the Soviets provided several thousand technicians for construction of a variety of industrial enterprises, including modern sugar mills, fertilizer plants, and an electric plant. Cubans also studied engineering, computer science, agriculture, construction, and food processing in the Soviet Union.

The reorganization efforts had a salutary affect upon the Cuban economy. Productivity and exports expanded. Cuban textiles, shoes, construction materials, metals, and pharmaceuticals found their way into the market. World sugar prices increased, which helped offset the decline in sugar production after 1970. In fact, the economy grew at a 5.7 percent annual rate between 1971 and 1980. Still, sugar remained Cuba's primary export, accounting for 65 percent of the total share in 1985, and the Soviet Union continued to underwrite the economy through debt postponement and extended credits. As late as 1986, a new agreement between Moscow and Havana provided for $3 billion in annual credits through 1990. Also, by 1986 the Soviets accounted for 64 percent of Cuba's exports and 62 percent of its imports. In economic terms, the Cuban Revolution had traded a colonial client status with the United States for one with the Soviet Union. But the new arrangement offered promises of national autonomy and, over time at least, limited development.

The combination of sustained economic growth and political stability, supported by the Soviets, enabled the Castro government to meet many of its egalitarian goals: redistribution of land, rent reduction, and the rationing of scarce goods. Private beaches, clubs, and schools were eliminated and resorts and luxury hotels opened to all Cubans. The 1963 social security law extended illness benefits to all workers and retirement to the totally incapacitated. Wages increased, especially in the agricultural sector.

A high-water mark in the political course of the Revolution also came in 1970. Government reorganization and a sense of democratization followed. In 1975, following its approval by top government officials, a draft of a new constitution was widely discussed in labor councils, local assemblies, CDR meetings, and in the media, where it received strong approval and where minor changes were suggested that, for the most part, were incorporated into the final document. In February 1976, the Cuban populace approved the new constitution. Modeled after the 1936 Soviet constitution, it was dedicated to the implementation of Marxist-Leninist concepts and recognized the leadership of Fidel Castro. The constitution laid out the institutional framework of national and local government and gave the state exclusive powers over foreign trade, the exploitation of domestic resources, and national economic planning. While it guaranteed citizens the right to work and to receive state sponsored health care and education, the constitution also empowered the state to regulate the activities of religious institutions, establish ownership over mass media, and to punish those who manifested beliefs contrary to Revolution. Finally, the constitution legitimized the PCC as the highest leading force of the society and the state, therefore subordinating the country's institutional character to the party's guidance.

The new constitution established 169 municipal assemblies, 14 provincial assemblies, and 1 national assembly. The municipal assemblies give the appearance of popular participation in government with the power of authority over schools, health services, cinema, sports facilities, and transportation enterprises within its boundaries. Municipal assemblies also assume responsibility over local enterprises, including retail operations, consumer services, and factories producing for local consumption. They also elect delegates to the provincial assemblies, who in turn elect delegates to the National Assembly, thus removing the populace from the direct electoral process. The authority of the municipal and provincial assemblies, however, is severely limited by the fact that they are empowered to implement the decisions made at the national level. Local initiatives are forbidden.

In 1986, the National Assembly had 499 members, roughly one for every 20,000 inhabitants. The assembly does not represent all Cuban people. In reality the elected delegates, who serve a five-year term, represent the Cuban communist elite. Despite the formal trappings of power—16 working committees to oversee the workings of the judiciary, transportation, industry, communications, and so on—the assembly meets for only a few days twice a year. It is not capable of formulating or debating legislation. Although the deputies do discuss certain economic and social problems and air some differences of opinion at assembly sessions, they do not resolve controversial policy differences. As the constitution provides, the National Assembly is bypassed on important decisions made by the Council of State.

As a delegate from Oriente Province, Fidel Castro has the right to speak on the Assembly floor. He does. He dominates the discussion, speaking more frequently and longer and on a broader range of topics than any other delegate. No one criticizes Castro. His proposals, whether for or against a measure, or to postpone it, have always been accepted.

From its own ranks, the National Assembly elects a 31-person Council of State. It technically functions as a cabinet, but also doubles as the standing legislature when the National Assembly is not in session. The Council is charged with issuing decree-laws, proposing legislation, and replacing ministers. Real power rests with the Council's President who, according to the constitution, is also head of state and government.

At the initiative of the President of the Council of State, the Assembly appoints a Council of Ministers which stands at the apex of the government structure and is the nation's highest-ranking executive and administrative organ. Its membership varies, usually between 35 and 45 members appointed and removed by the National Assembly at Fidel Castro's request. Fidel Castro is president of the Council, as well as formal head of state and government, thus holding Cuba's top executive and administrative positions. His brother Raúl is the council's vice president.

Technically accountable to the National Assembly, the Council of State is empowered to conduct foreign policy and trade, maintain internal security, draw up bills for submission to the National Assembly, and organize and conduct the political, economic, cultural, scientific, social, and defense activities outlined by the Assembly. The Council has an Executive Committee whose members control and coordinate the work of ministries and other central organizations.

The PCC became the vanguard of the Revolution and was charged with leading the effort toward the goals of the construction of a communist society. Thus, by the end of the 1970s the PCC was the primary political institution in the country. The PCC also practices this form of democratic centralism. In theory at least, the party members at the local level elect their own secretary and propose delegates to the party congresses, but that process is also tightly controlled from the top.

The party congress meets every five years, technically to discuss, change if necessary, and then approve policies set from above. For the interim periods, the party congress elects the Central Committee, which in turn elects a political bureau (politburo). In practice, however, nominations for positions of leadership are approved at the next highest level of party organization. In this way, what appears to be a bottom-up system of leadership, is in fact a system in which the leadership at the top perpetuates its own hold on power. Ultimate political power rests in the politburo, the top policymaking body of the PCC. Fidel Castro is both head of the PCC and president of the politburo. The politburo determines party policies and reviews legislation before it is proposed to the National Assembly. The Secretariat of the Central Committee is another important PCC institution. Usually comprised of 6 to 11 members, the Secretariat is concerned with internal party affairs, such as the assignment of personnel, and studies questions relating to party discipline and promotions. In theory, the Central Committee elects the party leaders who sit on the politburo, but in reality, the slate of candidates presented by Fidel Castro is customarily approved.

The Central Committee usually meets twice a year to respond to Castro's initiatives, although it appears to have never opposed him. Castro sets the agenda and the tone for the evaluation of party performance. For example, Castro, not the Central Committee, found the 1985 economic plan seriously deficient and appointed his own staff to revise it. Again, in 1987 and 1988 Castro provided the details of plans for the construction program, the machine industry, water conservation, agricultural development, bus transportation, and the augmentation of toothpaste production.

The rank and file party members are expected to give their unquestioned support of the party's objectives. In practice, this means that party members are charged with uncovering abuses, negligence, irregularities, and any other kind of deficiency in the work place. Effectively, the party member has become the chief instrument to assure the leadership's defined objectives in the workplace. Thus, when an enterprise is falling short of production quotas, the party member must encourage workers to volunteer for overtime to correct the shortcomings. He must hold meetings with the workers to educate them regarding the leadership's goals and objectives. As a result, the rank and file often find themselves in conflict with managers of business enterprises and the workers themselves.

Given the governmental and Communist Party structures, elections in Cuba do not represent the will of the people, despite Castro's gleeful statements about the fact that all Cubans 16 years of age and older are empowered to vote and do so, as indicated by the high voter turnout, usually 95–98 percent. As with the government and party structures, the electoral rights of the Cuban populace are greatly limited. Elections were not meant to provide a chance for people to select from competing candidates or policy alternatives. Instead, elections were designed to legitimize established institutions and to ratify the leadership's choice of both candidates and policies. Elections have not offered the Cubans the opportunity to vote among competing candidates or political parties. The only legalized party, the PCC, controls the nomination process, beginning at the mu-

nicipal level. There, the party and the government-sponsored mass organizations have the right to distribute political material and hold electoral
meetings. The party also approves the nominees, usually two per position
at the municipal level. However, they cannot familiarize the voters with
their opinions. Instead, the PCC prepares biographies, not position papers, of the candidates and posts them in public areas. The electorate then
chooses among the candidates, giving the appearance of a democratic
election. Once elected, the legislator takes an oath pledging to respect the
leading role of the PCC in Cuban affairs.

In addition to detailing the nation's political structure and legitimizing
the power of the PCC, the 1976 constitution provided for the establishment of a new court system composed of 1 people's Supreme Court, 14
provincial courts, and at the local level, 169 municipal or people's basic
courts. The constitution made the judiciary ultimately responsible to the
National Assembly. At each level, the corresponding local assembly
elects judges and is entitled to recall them. The Cuban Supreme Court is
not empowered to consider the constitutionality of laws; this function is
reserved for the National Assembly, a pattern consistent with Eastern Europe at that time. The 1976 constitution charged the court "to maintain
and strengthen the socialist legality"; to "safeguard the economic, social,
political regime" as established by the constitution; and "to increase the
citizen's awareness of their duty of loyalty to the homeland and the cause
of socialism." Under these conditions, the court system does not serve as
a check upon the other branches of government, nor does it concern itself
with the protection of individual rights and freedoms that could be curtailed by an all-powerful government. Military courts also exist, along
with some labor courts, but in both instances their function is to apply,
not interpret, the law of the land.

These changes were little more than cosmetic. Castro remained the
dominant figure as the Maximum Leader. The tightly knit leadership built
around Fidel Castro and his brother Raúl remained in tact and they continued to control policies and functions in Cuban society. There still was
no room for dissent; opposition was silenced in defense of the Revolution.
The masses continued to receive indoctrination of Marxism-Leninism in
formal classes at the workplace and in the neighborhood. Loyalty to the
Revolution was paramount. Castro remained master manipulator of public opinion and in the propagation of partial truths, which in the controlled media gave the appearance of reality.

In the process of reorganization, Castro focused upon the military's role
in defending the Revolution, not only abroad but at home. Headed by Raúl
Castro, the Revolutionary Armed Forces received generous allotments of

the national budget and became a modern and effective fighting unit. The Armed Forces loyalty to the maintenance of the regime was never in doubt.

During the 1970s Cuba's armed forces became more professional and modern in keeping with the institutionalization process. The army reassumed its traditional role of national defense, but its involvement in international missions demonstrated its offensive capabilities. The size of the military grew during the 1970s. Estimates including reservists reached as high as 600,000 men and women. Its officers, many trained in the Soviet Union and Eastern Europe, became highly skilled technicians and government administrators. During the 1970s, Cuba received arms transfers from the Soviet Union, estimated at $1.1 billion between 1976 and 1980 alone, including MiG-23 and MiG-27 fighter planes. The Soviets also sent technicians and military advisors to Cuba and trained Cuban military intelligence officers in the Soviet Union. A Soviet combat brigade of some 2,600 men remained in the country since the 1962 missile crisis. Soviet submarines periodically visited Cuban ports, particularly at Santiago. Cumulatively, the Cuban military became a formidable force, larger than any other in the Caribbean region. The officer corps remained loyal to Fidel Castro's leadership. Despite a selection process and educational program that inculcated loyalty to the Revolution, Communist Party cells throughout the ranks served as an insurance policy against any disgruntled officers or men.

As Castro moved to institutionalize the Revolution's political apparatus, he also placed new emphasis upon the mass organizations, such as the CDRs, the FMC, Asociación Nacional de Agricultures Pequeños (ANAP), and CTC. He expanded their roles in the formulation and implementation of policy. The organizations were directed to address local problems with a new sense of volunteerism.

The CDRs dated to 1960 and remained the most well-known, most notorious, and most inclusive of the Revolution's mass organizations. They continued to work with local law agencies and the PCC in sponsoring citizens meetings to express support for the regime's goals and objectives, organizing mass displays of support for the Revolution, such as attendance at Castro's speeches, and sanctioning demonstrations and political funerals. In addition, the CDRs performed a variety of civic functions, including the supervision of immunization campaigns, collecting recyclable materials, neighborhood beautification, and the like. It remains a neighborhood organization, recruiting all people loyal to the Revolution usually into groups of 60 people.

As much as to foster identification with the Revolution, a major purpose of the CDRs was to continue to intimidate persons hostile to the government. The CDRs acted as a vigilante group by reporting on dissenters and gathering information on individual loyalty. By the 1980s, for example, the CDRs passed judgment on more than 655,000 verifications concerning the political and social position of young men entering the military service. The CDRs also organized demonstrations against opponents of the government. In the spring of 1980, the CDRs organized demonstrations against those wanting to leave Cuba in the Mariel boatlift. Even relatives of those emigrating became targets of public abuse.

Another mass organization that dated to 1960 was the FMC, directed by Raúl Castro's wife, Vilma Espín. Eighty percent of Cuban women were FMC members by the mid-1980s. The FMC became an instrument for the government to communicate its objectives to women and to report women's needs to the government. The two-way communication resulted in the Maternity Law, the Family Code, the Protection and Hygiene Law, and the Social Security Law. The FMC formed health brigades to conduct programs in infant care, environmental hygiene, uterine cancer diagnosis, and health education. By 1986 the FMC had established 838 childcare centers throughout Cuba. With education now more accessible, women accounted for 50 percent of the university students and comprised 35 percent of the workforce by the early 1980s. Still, females remained underrepresented in key administrative, management, and government positions, a fact that Fidel Castro is mindful of. By the mid-1980s, FMC leaders became more forthcoming in their public criticism of many laws, regulations, and institutional practices which they considered detrimental to women's status in Cuban society, including discrimination in the workplace. The FMC was also concerned about the portrayal of women as sex objects, as illustrated in its 1985 criticism of the Cuban Tourist Institute for its depiction of women in their advertising.

The ANAP dated to May 1961 and by the mid-1980s was considered by many as the most effective of Cuba's mass organizations. Since the Agrarian Reform Law of 1959, the state began to collectivize farms as the small producers could not meet the government's production demands. The practice accelerated with the new economic policies agreed to in 1966. As a result of government purchases and acquisitions, the numbers of private small farmers decreased from approximately 250,000 in 1967 to 110,000 by 1981 and approximately 98,000 by 1989. By the mid-1980s, a Cuban government report indicated that 80 percent of the farmland was state owned, 12 percent was in cooperatives, and only 8 percent was privately owned. Still, the same report continued, the private farms outproduced the others in food consumed on the island.

In response to the farmers' demands and recognizing the need for expanded foodstuffs available in the cities, in 1980 the government permitted free farmer's markets. Here, farmers could sell their surplus at whatever the market would pay. Within two years, Castro became disturbed by the high prices and profits these markets generated. Castro proposed taxes to curtail both, but ANAP persuaded him to impose price ceilings instead. The measure proved only temporary, as profits continued to rise and enabled farmers to purchase cars and frequent hotels and restaurants. The urban public became increasingly discontent. In a countermove to the farmers, the government established a parallel market in 1983. These quasi-black markets made available many rationed foodstuffs at high prices and, of course, kept the profits. The urban consumer could afford little of the fresh produce and meats that both markets offered and placed the blame upon the private farmers.

ANAP found itself in conflict, not only with the frustrated consumers, but also Fidel Castro's vision of a socialist society. Castro believed that the private sale of food at market prices led to inequitable financial gains for a tiny minority and potentially threatened the state's loss of control over agricultural resources in general. In his battle over the private farmers, Castro utilized another segment of the farm population, the cooperative farmers, who also saw the private farmers as a source of greed. They had accepted greater state supervision of their farming, only to lose out to others. Confronted with consumer anger and disgruntled cooperative groups, and determined to retain state control over agriculture, in May 1986 Castro decreed an end to the free markets. Castro claimed that he was responding to the demands of the farmer's cooperatives. As the six-year program came to an abrupt halt, Castro set out to attack the private farmers. In May 1987 he appointed Orlando Lugo, a Central Committee member, to replace José Ramírez Cruz as head of ANAP. In turn, Lugo replaced many of the organization's subordinate officers. ANAP also lost its role in distributing credit and negotiating plan targets. These duties were assigned to other ministries.

Agriculture remained a problem in Cuba. The Frutas Selectas, the state agricultural agency that succeeded the free markets, was criticized for poor organization and inflexibility. Severe weather hindered crop growth from 1985 to 1987. While there was an increase in production of table vegetables by cooperatives for the 1964–87 period, ANAP reported that nearly one-third of the 1,700 state cooperatives operated at a loss.

The CTC lost its importance in the decade following Castro's march into Havana. It was reconstituted in 1970 as part of the institutionalization of the Revolution when the government supervised elections of

37,047 local sections that chose 164,367 officials to represent 2.2 million workers. Technically charged with representing the workers, in reality the institutionalized CTC ensured that workers were promoting society's collective interests rather than pursuing selfish, gain-oriented aims. In the early 1970s, Castro and his advisors defined the union objectives as: (1) support of the government; (2) participation in vigilance and defense activities; (3) cooperation in order to improve managerial efficiency; (4) maintenance of labor discipline; and (5) raising worker's political consciousness.

As designed, workers were consulted through assemblies about proposed laws, regulations, production goals, administrative matters, and the ratification of government measures affecting labor. In practice, however, the consultations were sporadic and workers' considerations and recommendations rarely made their way beyond union leaders at the plant level. As one high ranking union official explained, the assemblies rarely addressed the issue at hand, but rather were used by administrators to chastise workers for slacking off and were only concerned with enforcing workers' discipline. Castro concurred and in February 1980 decreed a law that stripped labor councils over control of worker discipline. Despite Castro's subsequent admission that the decree only abetted discontent in the workplace, the issue remained unaddressed in 1986. That same year, *Granma* characterized the failure to incorporate workers' suggestions into the planning process as one of the principle deficiencies of the Cuban economic system.

By the mid-1980s, Cuba pointed to notable achievements in education, nutrition, and health services. In education, a variety of programs brought the nation's literacy rate to 96 percent, a figure higher than many other Latin American countries. Primary and secondary school enrollments increased markedly to 3.3 million children in the mid-1980s. University enrollments expanded greatly beyond the pre-1959 levels, and the focus of education changed from the humanities, social sciences, and law, which prepared one for government positions, to the sciences, engineering, architecture, and agriculture to serve the larger needs of a socialist society.

In nutrition, a food rationing system set a target of 1,900 calories per capita daily intake in the early 1960s, but improved food production led to higher consumption. The United Nations reported that Cuba had reached a per capita daily intake of 2,705 calories by the early 1980s, above the generally recognized minimum of 2,500 calories. Not all of this could be attributed to the government programs. Workers also paid a small fare for lunches at the workplace, and gray and black markets offered food items otherwise unavailable. Gray markets enabled families to swap goods among themselves, and the black market provided goods at above controlled market prices.

On the eve of the Revolution, Cuba had one doctor per 1,000 residents. Approximately one-half of the 6,300 doctors departed the island between 1960 and 1963. The Cuban government addressed the problem in the 1970s, so that by 1984, Cuba counted one doctor for every 490 residents. The number of nurses, X-ray and laboratory technicians, anesthetists, and rehabilitation specialists also markedly increased. By the 1980s, the number of hospitals and clinics, both in general and in specialty fields, expanded significantly and spread across the breadth of the country. The island's hospitals and clinics also performed experimental and lifesaving surgery that attracted patients from around the world. Equally impressive figures were found in dental hygiene.

The U.S. embargo severely limited Cuba's access to medicines and it took a long time for Cuba to recover, but in the 1980s the nation produced 83 percent of its own pharmaceuticals. As a result of this effort, Cuba counted a significant decrease in infant mortality rates and death by communicable disease, but joined the ranks of industrialized nations in which the principal causes of death were heart disease, cancer, and stroke.

But all was not well in Cuba. The advances in education, nutrition, and health care were not matched with personal comforts. A severe housing shortage continued to exist since 1959. The housing shortage that existed at the time of the Revolution was exacerbated by an exploding birth rate that nearly doubled the population to 10 million by 1980. The diversion of construction materials to other projects such as hospitals, schools, and roads also contributed to the problem. Despite the public attention given to the construction of vast projects like Ciudad José Martí in Santiago, which was designed to house 50,000 residents, and Alamar East outside of Havana for 100,000, housing units still lagged by one million in 1980. The crisis worsened as older homes fell into disrepair for want of both capital and materials for improvements. Across the island, the government simply lacked the resources to keep them in a proper state of repair. So bad was the situation that a total of 25,000 houses collapsed in 1979 alone.

Other inequities also surfaced. With the return of material incentives in the 1970s wage disparities reappeared, but at a greater rate than in the 1960s. In addition, the workers who successfully earned bonuses like refrigerators and televisions in the 1970s enjoyed a higher standard of living than the less successful. At a higher level, government officials, union leaders, and high-level technicians came to enjoy valued goods and services, including automobiles, better housing, and vacations abroad. These inequities became more pronounced in the 1980s.

On a personal level, men refused to accept the changing role of women. The government attempted to legislate new social arrangements. The 1974 Family Code, for example, mandated that men share in household maintenance responsibilities. In practice, the older, macho culture persisted as men refused to yield to egalitarian imperatives from the government in matters of home and sexual relations. Women still found themselves discriminated against at home and in the workplace in the late 1980s. Professional advancement remained limited.

By the late 1970s, Castro's regime became well aware of its need for complete control of political dissent and the risk involved in overcontaining it. In 1979, Castro drew attention to the need to step up vigilance on manifestations of enemy activity by antigovernment deeds and words. One of the dangers of suppressing all dissent is that it can build up quietly and manifest itself when unexpected. That is exactly what happened on April 1, 1980, when a group of 14 Cubans who wished to leave the country crashed their way onto the compound of the Peruvian embassy and, in the process, killed two Cuban police guards. In a fit of anger, Castro removed the police guards from around the Peruvian embassy, a move that unexpectedly opened the floodgates. On the evening of April 5 and throughout the next day, some 10,000 Cubans flocked to the Peruvian embassy compound. Castro then announced that all who wanted to leave the country could. Thousands of Cubans flocked to government offices to obtain the necessary exit visas. After announcing that it could absorb 1,000 of these Cubans, Peru turned the issue over to the United Nations High Commissioner of Refugees. Subsequently, the United States agreed to take 3,500 of the 10,000; Venezuela and Spain, 500 each; Costa Rica and Canada, 300; and Ecuador, 200. An airlift program provided for the evacuation until Castro suspended it on April 18, 1980. Five days later he announced that boats could come from Florida to the port of Mariel to pick up relatives of Cubans living in the United States. The exodus became a stampede. Before Castro decided to end the boatlift on September 26, 1980, 125,262 refugees came to the United States. The total included an estimated 5,000 criminals, infirm, and mentally ill and, as discovered later, nearly 2,000 Cuban agents. Clearly, the crisis affirmed Castro's control over the emigration of Cubans to the United States.

While the root causes of the exodus rested with Cuba's economic plight, limited political system, and restricted civil rights, the more immediate causes were attributed to Castro's decision in early 1979 to permit Cuban exiles in the United States to visit their relatives on the island, and at the urging of the United States, he permitted direct flights from Miami to Havana. In 1979 and 1980 the U.S. visitors brought not only an estimated $100 million dollars in cash to Cuba, but also television sets and other appliances and gadgets, new clothes, and equally important, stories of prosperity and freedom in the United States.

The end of the Mariel boatlift did not end Cuba's internal problems or its concomitant dissent. By the mid-1980s, the concentration of political power in the Castro clique, the privileges granted to Communist Party members, and the failure of the revolution to achieve its lofty social and economic objectives contributed to a measure of discontent across the island.

In sum, the economic disparities, shortage of social services, limited employment opportunities, and widespread corruption contributed to a sense of lethargy—a lost commitment to the Revolution. Individualism replaced the collective good. The Revolution had stagnated.

Chapter 5

SOCIALISMO O MUERTE

In February 1986, at the Third Congress of the Communist Party, Fidel Castro unleashed an unexpected scathing attack upon the nation's economic and governmental performance during the recent past. He understood that the popular discontent across the island was based upon the concentration of political power in the Castro clique, the privileges granted to Communist Party members, and the failure of the Revolution to achieve its lofty social and economic objectives. These injustices prompted Castro to declare the nation's recommitment to the Revolution in 1986 through a "Rectification Program." Rectification reemphasized the primacy of the Communist Party and Castro's preeminent role in the decision-making process. The few market reforms in place were rescinded and a new emphasis on the collective good returned. Volunteerism again became the model for achieving new state-mandated goals.

Castro directed his first missive at the economy. While the macroeconomic indicators appeared positive, the country faced serious financial difficulties for spending and consuming beyond its means. Overall growth rates for the 1980–85 period were positive—7.3 percent in global social product and 8.8 percent in industrial production, For the entire 1965–84 period, Cuba saw a respectable 6.3 percent economic growth rate. In contrast, during the 1980s, the state budget deficit increased by 17 percent. In 1986, Cuba halted interest payments on its $3.5 billion debt to international creditors and reported a trade deficit of $520 million. Yet, Castro claimed that $1.2 billion in hard-currency imports was the "indispensable minimum" for the economy, at a time when hard-currency exports declined by $500 million. Cuba's ability to earn hard currency dramatically weakened in 1986. Hurricane Kate inflicted heavy damage across the island, world prices for oil and sugar markedly declined, and the U.S. dollar was devalued. The next year, 1987, the Cuban Central Bank reported a 3.5 percent decline in economic growth. Despite a new trade treaty with the Soviet Union that promised a 50 percent trade increase over the next five years, Cuban economists thought it would be insufficient to meet the challenge.

Castro placed responsibility for the poor economic performance at several doorsteps, starting with the SDPE, mandated by Moscow and implemented in 1976 as the price for Soviet economic support. SDPE encouraged limited market reforms, such as the farmer's markets, and expanded autonomy for state enterprises. But the emphasis upon individualism, Castro noted, deviated from the primacy of Castro's Revolution—a commitment to socialism.

Castro next detailed the problems in the workplace. Many of these problems were not new to Cuba. Work norms, or productivity schedules, were outdated, and salaries were not commensurate with output. Marginal production appeared to be a common practice, and it meant that many workers received a full day's pay for a half-day of work and then spent the afternoon seeking private gain. Oftentimes, managers hired skilled workers at wages higher than allowed by law. The net effect was an increase in the average wage from 148 pesos per month in 1980 to 188 pesos in 1985, which in turn fed the inflationary black market.

Despite a 1980 law to do so, management failed to enforce labor discipline and state regulations. The problem was compounded by the municipal courts where workers often won their appeals against management. In 1985, for example, of the approximately 32,000 appeals to municipal courts, only 38 percent confirmed administrative decisions. Reminiscent of the 1940s, unions appeared more powerful than management.

In addition, enterprises frequently ignored their own budgets and contractual obligations between enterprises. Management often inflated costs and prices to meet output in value, but at the same time paid little attention to quality control. The burdensome planning process ignored worker input. Nepotism and friendship prevailed in hiring and promotion; volunteerism declined; managers ignored public opinion as they steered state resources to their own gain. Those who reported problems in the workplace found themselves ostracized, not rewarded. In effect, these activities and processes ignored the national consciousness in favor of individual gain.

Concomitantly, the quality of life for the average Cuban deteriorated. The long-standing housing shortage significantly worsened, climbing 17 percent since 1971, from 754,000 housing units to 888,000 in 1985. Older homes fell into disrepair and utility services were severely strained. The deficit in childcare centers escalated between 1980 and 1985. For example, only 12 childcare centers were built in 1982, woefully short of the needs for 20,000 children. The shortage adversely impacted upon the government's ability to incorporate more women into the workforce. The demand for hospital beds also increased throughout the 1980s, most notably in Havana, but the construction of new hospitals dramatically lagged.

There were other problems. Education no longer served as the vehicle to a better life. Despite the mass literacy programs of the 1960s, the subsequent construction of schools across the island, and concomitant compulsory education, Cuban students and teachers suffered from a lack of supplies and textbooks. Geared to ensure the continued support of the Revolution, education stilted the student's thought processes. University education remained limited to the most meritorious students, meaning those who exhibited a commitment to the Revolution. But a university education did not guarantee appropriate employment in Cuba's ever-contracting economy. At the same time, the Revolution reserved places in medical school and in housing for successful international athletes, returning military veterans, and those expressing deep loyalty to the Revolution.

In addition, corruption plagued Cuban society. Highly placed government officials diverted government funds for importation of luxury goods from the West. Physicians accepted bribes in return for furnishing fraudulent medical certificates to help people evade state employment. In rural areas, "wildcat farmers" illegally cultivated thousands of hectares of land. The urban poor illegally claimed apartments and houses and tapped into unmetered electricity. Since the late 1970s, people made money by providing scarce products or services, by acting as retail distributors, or by diverting state-owned property to private use. Castro was well aware that inequality, privilege, and official corruption contributed to political disaffection elsewhere in the socialist world. He often used Poland as the model.

To correct the many problems confronting Cuba, in December 1986 Castro exhorted the Cuban people to recommit themselves to the Revolution. The reaffirmation of socialist values and the success of socialism in Cuba, Castro argued, would light the way for socialism everywhere. Castro emphasized the significance of Cuba's role as the standard-bearer for a vigorous socialism. National pride, hitched to socialist ideas, became the engine of *Fidelismo* in the 1980s and 1990s. Castro's exhortations came at a time when socialism elsewhere in the world was undergoing reform or retreat.

In fact, Castro's attempt at rectification became a crusade to save the
Cuban Revolution from forces beyond his control. The international
scene dramatically changed over the next 15 years, and those changes impacted adversely upon Cuba. Still, Castro clung to the past in order to
save his Revolution.

Reminiscent of campaigns during the 1960s, and reflecting Castro's
tendency to place responsibility for failure on others, in 1986 he lam-
basted bureaucrats and technocrats for not being able to understand the
needs of the populace. Managers tended to be indifferent, negligent, irresponsible, and reluctant to change. Political and administrative cadres,
not the workingmen, were principally responsible for the state of affairs
that necessitated rectification.

In application, rectification meant the dismantling of the institutionalization process begun in the 1970s, the downsizing of pragmatic decision
making, diminishing the role of the SDPE, and discontinuing market reforms, inserting, in their place, a call for a new national consciousness, or
concenia. Castro resurrected doctrinal orthodoxy. Rectification started
with measures designed to improve the economic and social conditions.
Decisions were issued in a series of plans from 1986 to 1989. No one escaped rectification.

Because the SDPE plan that transferred some of the responsibility for
economic management to enterprise managers and local political officials
had failed, Castro turned to the PCC to implement the economic direc-
tives. The Communist leadership repeated its claim to legitimacy on the
basis of their history and declared that they were the repository of the national honor and the popular well-being. And, as head of the PCC, Castro would direct the changes. They implicitly argued that only history
could pass judgment upon their exercise of power. Consequently, the PCC
could not be subjected to the supervision of elections. Through its contact
with the masses, the party served as its own check and balance. Also,
since the SDPE had lost contact with the masses, the party would now assume that role. The PCC mandated that provincial and municipal cadres
visit enterprises, schools, and neighborhoods to identify problems, provide solutions, and convey explanations. Regular institutional channels
often failed to feel the popular pulse. A vanguard party had to listen to ordinary Cubans, establish a dialogue with them, and gain their confidence.
In other words, the local party cadres were to lead, not administer.

The Rectification Program immediately threatened the job security of
those responsible for political work and economic management. According to a December 25, 1988, Granma article, over 400 administrative
cadres were removed from their positions, including over 130 directors of

enterprises or managers of factories. Similarly, over 85 grass roots party leaders, including 44 general secretaries, were removed from their posts before the end of 1986. A reevalution of work norms (production quotas), the creation of special elite worker units, and the merger of job categories resulted in greater discipline in the workplace. Using cost accounting methods resulted in more realistic workers norms, reducing the number of work norms to 500,000 in 1988 from the 3 million that existed in 1986.

The PCC also restored the old forms of labor mobilization. Microbrigades, formed in the 1970s as construction contingents and a volunteer work force, exemplified the reinforcement of politics to attain economic results. Their revival proved significant. Over 400,000 people volunteered to meet various social and economic tasks. In the first two years, the microbrigades built 111 day-care centers with a capacity for 23,000 children, 16,515 new homes, 1,657 medical facilities for the family/neighborhood doctor program, 9 polyclinics, 8 special schools, 32 bakeries, and the new Havana site, EXPOCUBA, for national and international fairs and exhibits. In addition, they were responsible for adding 300 new hospital beds to the system. The Ministry of Construction also added another 23,443 housing units.

At the same time, workers' salaries were adjusted. While the average salary remained about 188 pesos per month through 1988, workers in the productive sectors benefited over those in the service sectors. Castro reasoned that linking salaries to actual output would also increase the national consciousness. As a result, salary increases benefited 13,700 health and bakery workers, and an estimated 200,000 agricultural workers. In contrast, workers in public administration experienced a 3 percent decrease and those in industry and construction about 2 percent. In addition, by the end of 1988, the government laid off or transferred to productive work more than 6,300 administrative workers and 16,400 administrative cadres. Not all workers were pleased with the decisions and their consternation led to a charge by some that rectification meant an attack upon their income.

During the period of rectification, the government budget for basic social services increased by 7.3 percent and health care and education by 12.1 percent. Crime and juvenile delinquency were addressed with the 1986 National Commission for Crime Prevention and Social Assistance, and the 1987 penal code redefined 80 criminal activities to misdemeanors.

Rectification also addressed the mass media to ensure Castro's control over the dissemination of information. Reportedly, Castro once told a Western journalist that the media "must serve the Revolution." Since the 1960s, responsibility for the mass media rested with the Departamento Orientación Revolucionario (DOR) of the Communist Party's Central Committee. The regime controlled news reporting through the 3,000 member professional association of journalists, the Unión Periodistas de Cuba (UPEC). The official party newspaper, *Granma,* set the tone for how information should be presented to the public in less authoritative publications, such as *Bohemia, Juventad Rebelde, Trabajadores,* and *Mujeres.* All of Cuba's radio and television stations came under the control of the Instituto Cubano de Radiodifusion (ICRT), subordinate to the Ministry of Communications.

In 1985, the U.S. introduction of "Radio Martí" prompted Castro to refocus the direction of mass communications, especially to the young people. In June 1987 *Granma's* longtime editor, Jorge Enrique Mendoza, whose relationship with Castro dated to their days in the Sierra Maestra, was replaced by Enrique Román, a former lieutenant in the Cuban Fuerza Aérea Revolucionaria (FAR). In making the appointment, Castro directed Román to take a more sophisticated and intellectual approach to reporting the news. Castro also emphasized that criticism was not to be tolerated because Cuba remained in a "state of war."

Clearly, the fine arts, literature, and other expressions of popular culture came increasingly under the control of government bureaucrats. Castro wanted to prove that everything within the revolution was possible, but outside of it, nothing was. In so doing, Castro stifled creativity, artistic freedom, and individualism.

The success of the Rectification Program ultimately depended upon Castro's charisma, his ability to persuade the people to commit themselves to *patria* (fatherland), and the ideals of the socialist cause. He kept his hand on the pulse of the nation through a special commission to keep him fully abreast of domestic developments. The primacy of the PCC, and Fidel Castro in particular, remained. But it was also a litmus test for Castro as he became accountable for the shortcomings of rectification.

Not all sectors were pleased with the consequences of rectification. For example, Castro had to defend workers' protests about salary adjustments, but they did not accept his explanation that the adjustments were for the good of the nation. The common man continued to endure material shortcomings, and, in fact, lost access to many consumer goods because of the new economic restrictions. The government's closing of the farmer's markets not only curtailed the availability of foodstuffs, but also stifled a spirit of entrepreneurship in transportation and retail services. Amidst this continued sacrifice, special privileges remained for the chosen few, such as the successful athletes, the most loyal party members, and high government officials.

If the popular discontent was not enough to worry Castro, rectification's requirement for continued loyalty and honesty by high government officials was shattered in 1989. In June the government arrested Division General Arnaldo Ochoa, a Hero of the Republic, veteran of the wars in Ethiopia and Angola, and commander of the Western Army. Also arrested were the Interior Ministry's Colonel Antonio de la Guardia and 12 other high ranking and security officers. These 14 men of high prestige, valor, and impeccable credentials were charged with drug trafficking and endangering national security. Their arrest came at a time when international opinion called for strong condemnation of drug traffickers. In the end, Ochoa, Guardia, and two others were found guilty and sentenced to execution before a firing squad. The others received prison sentences ranging from 10 to 30 years. The purge did not end there. Interior Minister José Abrantes and several top security officers were dismissed along with dozens of other persons in other ministries. The broad sweep of dismissals led to speculation that Ochoa and Guardia were at the head of a clandestine movement against Castro, and the drug trafficking charges provided a neat cover for the serious threat to the Revolution.

In September 1989, the Communist Party implicitly recognized its own weaknesses. Using *Granma* as the vehicle, it declared that the Ochoa case was an exception to the loyalty and honesty of the national leadership. The party also recognized the need to address popular skepticism about the government by calling for *perfeccionamiento,* or the improvement of government institutions. Fidel Castro was more forceful when he demanded "*Socialismo o Muerte.*"

As Castro attempted to rectify the Revolution, events in the international arena adversely impacted Cuba. Throughout the 1980s, Cuba endured increasing U.S. political pressure. The Reagan administration came to office determined to pursue a confrontational policy toward Cuba. The Cuban American National Foundation (CANF), a nonprofit Miami-based organization founded by Jorge Más Canosa, an anti-Castro Cuban exile, supported the administration's policies. Until his death in 1997, Más Canosa had significant influence on U.S.-Cuban policy. He had direct access to Presidents Reagan, George H. W. Bush, and Bill Clinton, and, through CANF, helped finance several congressional candidates.

Reagan charged that the Soviet military and intelligence presence in Cuba directly threatened U.S. security. Thus, he demanded that Castro terminate his Soviet relationship, remove his troops from Africa and Grenada, and remove his support for the guerrilla forces in Central America. When Reagan arrived at the White House, he inherited the issue of Cuban military forces already in Angola and Ethiopia. To Reagan, this meant that Castro had larger designs upon Africa. And like President Carter before him, Reagan linked their removal as a precondition to normalization of relations. Castro refused to budge until a 1988 agreement among the belligerents paved the way for the removal of Cuban troops. By 1991, the Cuban troops came home, but their removal had little impact upon bilateral U.S.-Cuban relations.

Closer to home, Reagan challenged the Cuban presence in Grenada, where left-leaning Maurice Bishop seized power in 1979. By 1981, Bishop established relations with Cuba and accepted Castro's offer of arms, medical personnel, and technical personnel; a donation of fishing boats; and scholarships for Grenadian students to study in Cuba. Cuba's most important contribution was the attempt at construction of an airport at Port Salinas. Reagan charged that the airport would not only ferry Cuban troops to Africa, but also threaten U.S. interests in the Caribbean. In 1982, Reagan also charged that Grenada received unknown quantities of Soviet bloc military assistance. Amidst these developments, Bishop increased his anti-U.S. rhetoric.

Reagan was determined to sever the Bishop-Castro connection, but he needed a pretext to take action. In the turmoil that followed Bishop's assassination on October 18, 1983, Reagan announced the immediate need to rescue U.S. students enrolled at a local medical school whose security was allegedly threatened by conditions on the island. As Operation Urgent Fury unfolded some East European arms cache's were found. It also was verified that 748 Cuban nationals were on the island prior to the attack, but only 43 were military personnel. As the bodies of the Cubans killed in Grenada arrived at Havana's José Martí International Airport, a visibly distraught and dejected Fidel Castro met them. Castro wondered if Cuba was to be the next site of a U.S. invasion.

Ironically, in the 1990s, the United States gave scant attention to the reestablished diplomatic relations between Cuba and Grenada, the exchange visits between Castro and Grenada's Prime Minister, Keith Mitchell, and the ongoing Cuban projects in Grenada. Clearly, Castro no longer appeared as a threat to the Caribbean region.

In the meantime, however, Reagan confronted Castro over events in Central America, a region plagued, in varying degrees, by civil conflict since the 1970s. In July 1979, the Marxist-leaning Frente Sandinista Liberación Nacional (FSLN) toppled the Somoza regime in Nicaragua, and the Marxist-orientated Farabundo Martí Liberación Nacional (FMLN) appeared to be near victory in El Salvador.

FSLN leaders visited Cuba in the late 1960s to ascertain Castro's guerrilla strategy and, in the 1970s, received Cuban arms and welcomed its military advisors. As late as mid-1979, FSLN leaders visited Cuba and accepted Castro's advice not to accept Carter's mediation effort to end the conflict. Victory was in sight. By the time Ronald Reagan took over the presidency in January 1981, the FSLN was entrenched in power in Nicaragua and the Salvadoran guerrilla approached a high-water mark. The Reagan administration placed this conflict within its East-West prism: this was a communist plot to overtake Central America. Unless it was stopped, Secretary of State, Alexander Haig, threatened to go to the source—meaning Cuba. While the Cubans did provide advisors and matériel, the extent of the commitment has yet to become public, except to note that it declined after 1982. To intimidate both Fidel Castro and the rebels in Central America, Reagan ordered massive military maneuvers in the Caribbean. Reagan also rejected Castro's overtures in 1982 and 1983 to assist with the mediation of the Central American conflict.

As the war sputtered throughout the remainder of the 1980s, the Cubans and Soviets continued to supply the Salvadoran guerrillas, at least through 1988, at which time each claimed to have terminated their assistance, assertions rejected by the George H. W. Bush administration. Although anxious to get out of the Central American quagmire, the Bush administration, at best, was a reluctant supporter of the peace initiative by Costa Rican President, Oscar Arias, that brought an end to the conflict in 1992. By then, the Cuban connection to the isthmus had been severed and the Soviet Union had collapsed.

Until Castro severed his Moscow connection and ended its international adventurism, something the Reagan administration did not expect, there was no basis for discussion of other issues. Given this precondition, secret talks between Secretary of State, Alexander Haig, and Cuban Vice President, Carlos Rafael Rodríguez, in Mexico City in November 1981, and talks between Special Ambassador Vernon Walters and Castro in Havana in March 1982, went nowhere. Reagan also rejected Castro's subsequent offers to discuss the normalization of relations through the Spanish and Costa Rican governments. Following the conclusion of an Immigration Agreement in December 1984, Castro made a direct appeal to the United States to discuss all outstanding issues. Again, the Reagan administration refused. Castro's overtures were made to a U.S. president who believed that Cuba's economic strangulation would result in Castro's downfall.

On the economic front, the Reagan administration was determined to more stringently enforce the embargo against Cuba. Using the Trading with the Enemy Act as the vehicle, U.S. citizens were prevented from using dollars or U.S. bank credit cards when paying for expenses in Cuba, a move that severely contracted the tourist industry. In 1986, the administration began to closely monitor third country operations that arranged travel and goods to make their way to Cuba. In addition, visits by Cuban citizens to the United States were strictly controlled. The Reagan administration also sought to obstruct or sabotage Cuba's debt negotiations with Western creditors, to deny Cuba access to Western capital for financing development projects, and to pressure allies not to sell merchandise to, or purchase goods from, Cuba. All of this was done to limit the ability of Castro's government to earn badly needed hard currencies required to grow the Cuban economy and, in turn, foment internal political protest.

The Reagan effort met with failure. Western bankers were more impressed with Cuba's debt repayment record, its desire to expand trade with the Western nations, and the continuance of Soviet economic guarantees to Cuba. Reagan also failed to curtail Western trade with Cuba; it grew from an estimated $1 billion in 1975 to an estimated $1.8 billion in 1983. Only the plummet in the world price of sugar in the late 1980s denied Cuba hard currency, which in turn curtailed its trade with, and ability to gain credits from, the industrial world.

By 1987, most analysts concluded that U.S.-Cuban relations were at their lowest point since the 1962 missile crisis. The situation did not change with new President George H. W. Bush, who, in fact, raised the bar for normalization of relations. Bush called for the holding of free elections, the establishment of a market economy, and a reduction in the country's armed forces as preconditions to the normalization of relations. These conditions differed significantly from Presidents Jimmy Carter and Ronald Reagan, both of whom focused upon changes in Cuban foreign policy. Castro, who was not prepared to abandon his authority, again found a nonreceptive audience in Washington to his proposals for a discussion of issues that separated Cuba and the United States.

In addition to making what appeared to be impossible demands upon Castro, Bush also pursued a multitrack policy in an effort to destabilize his regime. Military maneuvers were stepped up in the Caribbean region. Increased funding for propaganda attacks upon Castro's dictatorship and Cuba's lack of human and civil rights were described to the public at home and in international forums. In 1992 Bush increased funding for "Radio Martí" and "TV Martí," despite clear evidence of their ineffectiveness. Bush also continued to emphasize the isolation of Cuba from the hemisphere by preventing its readmission to the OAS. But it failed in its bid to keep Cuba from being elected to the United Nations Security Council in 1989. In that instance, all Latin American states supported Cuba's candidacy because they no longer considered Castro a threat to the hemisphere.

The relationship between Cuba and the United States over Central America had wider implications. It became entangled with Cuban-Soviet relations after Mikhail Gorbachev became General Secretary of the Soviet Union in 1985. He clearly understood that the highly centralized state-run Soviet system failed to meet the needs of the Soviet people and greatly limited Soviet foreign policy options. In essence, Gorbachev wanted to end the Cold War. In so doing, he attempted to persuade Presidents Reagan and Bush to end the U.S. embargo on Cuba, but his plea fell on deaf ears. Gorbachev also ended Soviet support for revolutionary movements around the world. Its retreat from Central America did not sit well with Castro, who viewed the events on the isthmus as an extension of his own Revolution. Nor did Castro appreciate the possibility of facing the United States alone in the Caribbean region.

The Soviet-Cuban relationship, which had never been close, ended, not over Gorbachev's foreign policy direction, but by his implementation of *perestroika* (restructuring of economic and political institutions) and *glasnost* (freedom of expression) reforms at home. The unintended consequence of Gorbachev's programs was the collapse of the Soviet Union and the end of its stranglehold over Eastern Europe, events that recast the Soviet Union's special relationship with Cuba.

Gorbachev signaled Castro about changes in the relationship during his state visit to Havana in April 1989. Speaking before the Cuban National Assembly, Gorbachev said that it was essential to keep pace with the times rather than continue down the path of stagnation. Socialism needed "a new face" to adjust to the realities of the day. He told Castro and the Cubans that the Soviet economic relationship would have to reflect the new realities. Publicly, Castro was unmoved. He remained committed to his brand of socialism and reminded Gorbachev of his country's historic commitment to the island. Subsequently, the Soviet economic ministries were directed to devise plans that would put economic relations with Cuba on a more equitable basis. In effect, the new world order meant that Cuba would have to pay its own way. The loss of privileged market access and economic subsidies from the Soviets would prove disastrous to the Cuban economy.

Castro understood the significance of the forthcoming changes in the Soviet-Cuban relationship, yet, he reacted with a childlike petulance. He directed that English replace Russian as the required foreign language of study in schools. In ordering the change, Castro pointed out that there were no literary masterpieces or major scientific journals in Russian. And for the Cubans who received their university degrees in the Soviet Union, there were fewer government jobs. Castro also pointed out that, over the years, Cuba may have taken cheap Soviet oil, raw materials, basic industrial machinery and equipment, foodstuffs, consumer goods, and military aid, but for the more sophisticated needs that supplied its pharmaceutical factories, hospitals, and biotechnological center, Cuba shopped in Germany and Japan. Cuba earned the hard currency to do so by reselling refined Soviet crude oil and its biotechnological and pharmaceutical products to the Western Europeans and Latin Americans.

The relationship unraveled in 1991. Early that year, Gorbachev ordered the withdrawal from Cuba of the 3,000 Russian troops stationed there and later announced that future arms transfers would be on a commercial basis. Such actions signaled an end to the guarantee of Cuba's security.

With the collapse of the Soviet Union in August and September 1991, editorials in the Cuban Communist Party newspaper, *Granma*, indicated Castro's commitment to stay the communist course. Events in Moscow were described as a tragedy, and the Communist Party claimed that no matter what followed, Cuba would not deviate from the path it was on. The editorials also asserted that the Soviets sold out Cuba to the North Americans and, in so doing, compromised Cuban security and gave the United States a green light to carry out its long-standing plans of aggression against the island. Castro was no longer important to Moscow in its relationship with Washington.

In a terse statement on December 26, 1991, the Cuban Foreign Ministry noted only the formation of the Commonwealth of Independent States and that Cuba recognized them as independent republics. The Union of Soviet Socialist Republics (USSR) no longer existed. Cuba could only hope that the ties developed during the previous 30 years would continue. They did not. No other country came forward to prop Castro's Revolution.

As the Soviet relationship was changing, the Fourth Congress of the Cuban Communist Party convened in October 1991. This was the first congress at which not all votes were unanimous and there was debate on several issues: farmer's markets, crime, the electoral system, and the press. Many observers thought that the door finally had been opened to discussion, divergence of opinion, and criticism. Membership in the Central Committee underwent substantial change, with new persons constituting 60 percent of the total 225 members. The Council of State also underwent a 50 percent personnel turnover. In 1992 the National Assembly ratified party recommendations to provide for direct popular vote to elect provincial delegates and assembly deputies.

However, those who anticipated a change in the system left Havana disappointed. Castro did not want to repeat Gorbachev's fate. He was not going to weaken the Communist Party. Thus, at Castro's insistence, the

Congress confirmed that Cuba would remain a one-party state, committed to socialism, and that Cuba would prevail against U.S. aggression. Castro remained the ultimate decision-maker.

But the Congress was equally realistic when it anticipated future economic difficulties. The Congress recognized that there would be further cuts in electricity, transportation, and other services, which called for finding new foreign markets and committing to joint ventures with foreign enterprises to help develop the Cuban economy. The Congress also directed the party to be more in touch with the people by providing for the direct election of candidates to the provincial assemblies. This action deviated from Castro's long-standing insistence of the party's inviolability.

The loss of its major trading partner threatened to undo all the progress Cuba had made during 30 years of Castro's Revolution. Soviet oil and oil by-products, which the Soviets had made available to Cuba at prices below those in the world market and which accounted for nearly all the island's energy needs, decreased by 90 percent in 1993. Other key Soviet imports declined drastically: fertilizers by 80 percent; animal feed supplies by 70 percent. Imports of capital grade consumer goods, grains, foodstuffs, raw materials, and spare parts ceased altogether. Commercial relations with the Soviets declined from $8.7 billion in 1989 to $7.6 million in 1993, and trade with Eastern Europe nearly ended. In addition, Eastern European merchant fleets refused to carry goods to or from Cuba unless paid for in hard currency. The world market even militated against Cuba: world oil prices rose while sugar prices fell.

As the 1990s progressed, Castro confronted issues reminiscent of the 1960s: the worsening economic conditions on the island were accompanied by increasing U.S. hostility, and the Bush administration understood the adverse impact that the Soviet and East Bloc collapse had upon Cuba's ability to earn hard currencies. Bush used this condition to speak forcefully about tightening the economic noose, but instead, took only steps that had high publicity value. He prevented AT&T from connecting its newly laid $7 million underwater telephone cable connecting Cuba to the United States because it meant the transfer of approximately $220,000 in user's fees annually to Cuba. In 1991, he denied ABC Television the right to broadcast the Pan American Games from Havana because the payout to Cuba was $6 million. Bush, however, did not move against U.S. subsidiaries operating in third countries under the host country's legal system because of the problems in implementing such legislation and the difficulties such efforts could have on U.S. bilateral relations with the host countries. In contrast, several members of congress criticized Bush for not going further and proposed amendments to various bills providing for an end to the practice of U.S. subsidiaries in third countries from trading with Cuba.

Equally disappointed with Bush's position was CANF Chairman Jorge Más Canosa who pressured congressional sympathizers, including Senator Bob Graham (D., Fla.) and congressman Robert Torricelli (D., N.J.), both of whom represented large Cuban American communities. Graham and Torricelli cosponsored the legislation in congress that eventually became the Cuban Democracy Act (CDA). As it worked its way through the legislative process, the European Union, Canada, and even Latin American governments sympathetic to the political isolation of Cuba made their objections known. So, too, did the Bush administration. On September 22, the Senate approved the bill by voice vote and, two days later, the House by a 276–135 margin, but the CDA remained without Bush's signature when the 1992 presidential campaign began.

Más Canosa then approached the Democratic Party's presidential candidate, Bill Clinton, in spring of 1992, after which Clinton came out in favor of the CDA. Bush was equally self-serving in his newfound support for the CDA, particularly after his advisors found a loophole in the law. The CDA allowed the president to suspend provisions of the law when national security was at stake. In application, it meant that a diplomatic confrontation with Europe, Canada, and Latin America could be avoided. Bush signed the bill into law on October 23, 1992, in Miami before a large gathering of mostly Cuban Americans. Conspicuous by their absence were the bill's cosponsors, Bob Graham and Robert Torricelli.

The Torricelli Bill, as the CDA is popularly known, threatened to strangle Castro's Revolution, now near economic collapse. The bill prohibited subsidiaries of U.S. companies located in third countries from trading with Cuba, banned ships that departed from a Cuban port from stopping in the United States for six months before or after leaving Cuba, authorized the curtailment of aid to nations that provided assistance to Cuba, and allowed the Treasury Department to fine companies that violated the embargo up to $50,000 and to seize their property.

Almost unnoticed at the time, CDA's Track II provided for people-to-people contacts, including increased contacts between Cuban Americans and their relatives on the island, the donation of food directly to Cubans or Cuban nongovernmental organizations, export of medicines and medical equipment (but only with on-site inspection of deliveries in Cuba to avoid re-exportation), and the allocation of funds to nongovernmental bodies "for the support of individuals and organizations to promote nonviolent change" in Cuba. Such measures threatened to undermine the pillars of the Cuban Revolution.

Castro understood both the economic and humanitarian intentions of the Torricelli Bill. He denounced it as an act of U.S. aggression and an interference in Cuba's internal affairs.

From the start of his presidency in January 1993, Bill Clinton sent mixed signals regarding his position on Cuba. On the one hand he used the national security loophole to avoid implementation of the CDA. On the other hand, pressured by the congressional Cuban Lobby and CANF, Clinton withdrew the nomination of Cuban-born New York lawyer Mario Baeza to be Assistant Secretary of State for Inter-American Affairs and replaced him with Alexander Watson, a career diplomat who favored a hard line on Cuba, including continuation of the embargo, the political isolation of Cuba, and the demand for democratic government on the island. Other policy advisors who shared Watson's view included Richard Nuccio, Michael Skol, and Dennis Hays. Those within the administration advocating a change in policy included National Security Advisor, Sandy Berger, and his NSC colleagues Richard Feinberg and Maurice Halperin. From the start, Clinton and Watson publicly stated that there would be no change in Cuban policy. The hardliners prevailed, partly because U.S. policymakers mistrusted Castro's overtures based upon his historic record, and partly because Berger and his colleagues failed to define exactly what Castro should do or what the U.S. calibrated responses should be.

The mistrust of Castro led Clinton to ignore the suggestion from the president of the Cuban National Assembly, Roberto Alarcón, that the United States suspend its embargo for a 12-month period to encourage changes in the Cuban political process. Clinton also ignored the suggestions from Cuban moderates, including Eloy Gutiérrez-Menoyo, to relax the embargo because of the hardships it created upon the Cuban people during this "Special Period." In an effort to further strangle the Cuban economy, diplomats abroad were instructed to jawbone their host governments to stop trading with Cuba and new travel restrictions were placed upon exiles traveling from the United States to Cuba.

In contrast, the Clinton administration clamped down on the covert operations of the exile group Alpha 66, permitted Undersecretary of State for Political Affairs, Peter Tarnoff, to hold secret conversations with Alarcón in April 1995 in New York and Toronto, and clearly indicated that he would veto the Cuban Liberty and Democratic Solidarity Act (popularly known as the Helms-Burton Bill) if the congress approved the measure. The administration also developed a plan to expand academic, cultural, and people-to-people exchanges within the framework of CDA's Track II. By mid-1995 Clinton observers noted that the hardliners—Watson, Skol, and Hays were being marginalized in the making of Cuban policy and that the president seemed to be distancing himself from CANF.

As Clinton's policy wavered, the end of the Cold War brought Castro's experiment to near death. Scarcities of food, medicine, and consumer goods spread. The continuing decline in industrial and agricultural production caused by shortages of fuel, spare parts, and shipping added to a vicious cycle. The consequences proved staggering. By 1993 an estimated 50 percent of the industrial plants suspended operations. Factory closings, production declines, and transportation difficulties led to the displacement of nearly 20 percent of the population. Publication of books dropped by 50 percent. Work animals replaced machines in agriculture as the sugar crop dropped from 8.1 million tons in 1991 to 4.2 million tons in 1993.

The social consequences of economic scarcity were devastating. At times, rationing failed to provide sufficient food for a two-week period; nearly 300 medicines disappeared from circulation. World attention was drawn to the island in 1993 when some 50,000 Cubans suffered optic neuropathy due to a deficiency of Vitamin B complex. Abortions increased; for every 10 live births, there were an equal number of abortions. By the end of 1992, nearly 40 percent of bus and train schedules had been suspended, and taxi service all but disappeared. In 1994, nearly 700,000 Chinese-made bicycles had been distributed. Imposed blackouts shut down refrigeration and cooking facilities for hours at a time.

Castro's reaction to the problems was predictable. He placed responsibility everywhere except upon himself. Castro denounced the Soviet abandonment of communism and asserted that Cuba would go it alone, that it had a responsibility to demonstrate to the world that socialism could succeed. And as in the past, Castro again summoned the Cuban people to greater heroism and courage. Across the country, on streets and highways, in schools and at workplaces, billboards and posters alluded to Antonio Maceo's refusal to surrender at Baraguá to the Treaty of Zanjón in 1878. The nation was called upon to endure a new period of austerity. Castro proclaimed this to be a "Special Period" that necessitated new rationing schedules. Foods of all kinds became increasingly scarce, prompting the organization of urban workers into agricultural brigades in an effort to increase food production.

In addition to the reminders of past exhortations, new strategies had to be devised. Foreign investment was attracted through joint ventures, profit sharing, profit repatriation, and tax exemption. As a result, Australian, British, Canadian, Chilean, Mexican, and Spanish firms expanded into telecommunications, pharmaceuticals, construction, transportation, food processing, textiles, and mining. By the mid-1990s, the number of foreign firms operating in Cuba increased fourfold since 1987 to 500 firms. Cuba also expanded its commercial relations and sources of foreign exchange by concluding agreements with China, North Korea, Vietnam, Italy, and Jordan. They agreed to purchase Cuban sugar and tobacco, and in exchange, Cuba agreed to purchase their pasta, grain, chemical fertilizers, detergents, and medicines. The governments of Brazil, Chile, and Mexico extended credit lines.

The most extensive changes came in the tourist industry, which became a prime source of badly needed hard currency. Spaniards, Germans, and Austrians engaged in joint ventures with the Cuban government to build and operate facilities at Varadero, Camagüey, and Cayo Coco. Niche markets were developed in eco-, medical, and scientific tourism. Nightclubs opened to provide evening entertainment.

Tourism proved to be a double-edged sword. While the expanded tourist industry brought in the badly needed hard currency, it created animosity among the Cubans as foodstuffs, gasoline, and medicines were readily available to the dollar-spending tourists. The beaches, nightclubs, and consumer goods were out of reach for the average Cuban; the Cuban peso had no value in the tourist zones, as hard currency, especially the U.S. dollar, was accepted as legal tender. Prostitution flourished, and the government appeared to ignore the problem. Teachers, office workers, engineers, architects, and the like took jobs as servants, taxi drivers, bellhops, porters, busboys, and waiters to get tourist dollars. The mass infusion of dollars also contributed to an inflationary spiral. On the booming black market, the exchange rate leapt from 10 pesos per dollar to 100 pesos per dollar.

While the government sought long-term solutions, it improvised with short-term measures, including the "dollarization" of the economy which created new problems for Castro. In September 1993 the Council of State ended the state monopoly on employment, production, and distribution by authorizing self-employment in more than 50 trades and services. Under the law, automobile mechanics, taxi drivers, photographers, hairdressers, carpenters, cooks, and computer programmers, among others, were authorized to operate businesses and offer their services to the public at competitive prices. Artisans also were allowed to sell their works directly to the public for pesos or dollars. By mid-decade nearly 20,000 individuals had obtained self-employment licenses. In September 1994 the government authorized farmers to sell their surplus production on the open market after the quota for state markets was met. By the end of the year, nearly 150 farmer's markets appeared across the island. Homeowners opened small restaurants on their premises and rented rooms to travelers.

The ever-worsening economic and social conditions, along with the continued political repression, prompted a new wave of emigration. Recognizing that it could relieve the discontent by permitting migration, Castro permitted the easing of travel restrictions. In the early 1990s, an estimated 13,000 Cubans gained permanent U.S. residency by entering on visitor's visas, and countless others came through third countries. But it was the *balseros* (rafters) who drew most attention. Between 1990 and 1993 approximately 10,000 émigrés came across the Florida Straits in anything that floated. It became a deluge in August 1994 after Fidel Castro announced that his government would no longer interdict or hinder the departure of Cubans wishing to leave for the United States. Before it ended on September 9, 1994, an estimated 36,000 Cubans made their way to the Florida coastline. Countless others died at sea.

True to his pattern, Castro did not blame the exodus on Cuba's failed economy or the government's political repression, but instead, blamed the United States for causing the problem. Castro explained that the lax U.S. enforcement of its coastline, failure to honor the 1984 migration agreement to permit 20,000 Cubans to legally enter the United States annually, and its policy of granting automatic residency after 12 months encouraged the illegal immigration and the law breaking in Cuba.

As the number of *balseros* increased in August, the Clinton administration wrestled with policy options. Not wanting a repeat of the 1980 Mariel experience the administration announced on August 18, that all interdicted *balseros* would be detained at Guantánamo Naval Base until the Immigration and Naturalization Service (INS) determined their status. Furthermore, Cubans picked up at sea would not be allowed to enter the United States without first returning to Cuba and applying for an immigration visa or refugee status at the U.S. Interests Section in Havana. On August 20, Clinton banned charter flights from Miami to Havana and scaled back the quarterly remittances to Cuban families from exiles in the United States from $300 to $150 quarterly. On August 21, the White House announced that the administration was considering a blockade of Cuba. The Clinton administration also used the United Nations as a forum to focus upon human rights violations in Cuba. As the Guantánamo Bay naval facility became overcrowded, the United States began the transfer of refugees to Panama where President Ernesto Peréz Balladares agreed to house up to 10,000 Cuban émigrés at Howard Air Force Base.

The crisis ended with an accord reached in New York City on September 9, 1994. The United States agreed to accept 20,000 legal Cuban immigrants per year, the same as provided for in the 1984 migration agreement, in return for a Cuban promise to prevent its citizens from fleeing Cuba on rafts or other vessels. Cuba also agreed to allow the refugees at the Guantánamo Naval Base and in Panama to return home without reprisal. The $150 quarterly remittance and ban on charter flights to Cuba from the United States remained in effect.

The most important part of the agreement terminated the 28-year-old U.S. policy granting immediate residency to Cubans intercepted at sea and replaced it with their immediate repatriation or their detention at Guantánamo. Henceforth, the Cubans would have to reach the U.S. mainland to be secure from repatriation to Cuba. In 2000, the new policy contributed to the public outcry surrounding the Elían Gonzalez case.

In the meantime U.S.-Cuban relations continued to play out like a soap opera. On February 24, 1996, Cuban MiG fighter planes shot down two single engine Cessna 357 aircraft flown by a Miami exile group, Brothers to the Rescue (BTTR), for allegedly violating Cuban airspace. Four airmen were killed, while one plane and its pilot, José Basulto, returned to Florida. Since its founding in 1994, the BTTR became increasingly confrontational. It encouraged the growing civil disobedience in Cuba as a means of toppling Castro. That approach seemed to be gaining popularity among younger Cubans. Castro understood the threat, and the week before the shootdown he ordered the cancellation of the dissidents' meetings and the arrest of several of its leaders. Castro also warned the BTTR to stop its illegal flights over Cuba to airdrop antigovernment propaganda and clearly indicated that he would take all necessary measures to prevent such flights in the future. At the time, many analysts suggested that BTTR should have taken heed of Castro's crackdown and warning.

Amidst the public outcry against the shootdown in the United States, Clinton immediately called for a tightening of the Cuban embargo. Congressional hardliners obliged by completing the Helms-Burton legislation, which had languished in congress since September 1995. Clinton signed the measure on March 12, 1996.

Title III of the law allows former U.S. owners of nationalized property in Cuba to sue foreigners who invested (trafficked) in those enterprises in U.S. courts and prevents countries that purchase Cuban sugar, molasses, or syrups from reselling them or their derivatives in the United States. In addition, officers and stockholders of foreign companies trafficking in the confiscated properties would be denied future U.S. entry visas.

Congress stripped the president of the right to unilaterally lift the trade embargo, in place since 1962, by establishing a number of preconditions that Castro must first meet. These include the dismantling of the state security apparatus, freeing of political prisoners, legalization of political op-

position groups, international monitoring of free elections, and the withdrawal of Fidel and Raúl Castro from the process. The only leeway
granted the president was the right to suspend the implementation of certain clauses for up to six months when U.S. national interests are at risk.
In effect, the hardliners in congress seized control of U.S. policy toward
Cuba.

Most of the world already sympathized with Castro's charges against
the U.S. imposed embargo, but the protest reached new heights after the
passage of the Helms-Burton Bill because it implied the extraterritoriality
of U.S. law. The Canadian, European, and Mexican governments, whose
industries had already invested heavily in Cuba, including many former
owned U.S. properties, threatened to take the problem to the World
Trade Organization (WTO) and, at the same time, put in place retaliatory
measures should the United States implement this section of the Helms-
Burton Bill. Castro was delighted by the response from the international
community.

The U.S. business community, which had been relatively silent throughout the congressional proceedings, suddenly expressed vehement opposition
to Title III. U.S. business leaders pointed not only to its lost opportunities in
Cuba, but also to the adverse impact it would have upon their relationships
and investments in other countries. Every six months for the remainder of
his administration, Clinton continuously suspended Title III in order not to
damage U.S. national interests.

Overlooked at the time were the bill's provisions that the United
States would provide up to $8 million to assist with the democratization
of the island through reforming government institutions and assisting
with elections, a proviso approved by the European Union (EU) in 1997
when it adopted a binding resolution to pressure Castro to improve his
human rights record as a condition for future economic assistance. Castro
denounced the EU for succumbing to U.S. pressure. He also dispatched
diplomats throughout the Caribbean and Latin America to denounce the
continuing U.S. embargo and to assert that they could be the next victims
of U.S. aggression. Obviously, Castro had not lost sight of his historic
nemesis.

Still, the Helms-Burton Bill signaled that anti-Castro hardliners controlled a U.S. policy committed to bringing Castro down by economic
strangulation.

Despite the tightened U.S. embargo, Cuban statistical data from 1995
to 1997 shows that the Cuban economy did improve. Cuba's official 1998
portrait described the nation's political and social stability, illustrating its
slow but real progress after the economy all but collapsed between 1989

and 1994. Tourism and mining were booming, and foreign investment flowed into the energy sector, telecommunications, shipyards, and other industries. The Internet reached Havana, direct dial telephone service to the United States from major hotels opened, and two fast-food restaurants opened, Burgi and Rapido.

Yet, the hardships increased for the Cuban people. The United Nations reported that hunger and child malnutrition reappeared on the island. There was a deficit production in sugar cane and other state run agricultural pursuits, and continued shortages in consumer goods, medicines, housing, and cooking fuel. When these items were available, it was only at rising prices. A poll carried out secretly by academics from Mexico's University of Guadalajara in January 1998 showed that 76 percent of Cubans believed that life had gotten tougher, not better, during the previous year. Petty crimes, prostitution, and burglaries increased, and reports of cattle rustling surfaced. During this same time period, Cubans became more open in their criticism of Castro and his regime. By the mid-1990s, an estimated 50 dissident groups appeared across the island. Antigovernment demonstrations erupted in Cojímar and Regla in 1993 and in Havana in 1994. In the spring and summer of 1997 a series of bombings ripped through Havana's tourist hotels. The government denounced the protests and reacted harshly with harassment and arrests. As the Revolution approached its fortieth anniversary in 1999, Castro's earlier promises of a better life for all Cubans remained a distant dream.

Through it all, Fidel Castro continued to hold considerable authority and personal popularity. At the Fifth Communist Party Congress in October 1997, Castro clearly indicated that as long as he remained healthy and capable of discharging responsibilities, there would be no change in Cuba and, when that time arrived, his brother Raúl would be his successor. The congress approved. It was the first time in the history of the Revolution that succession was discussed. Still, as determined at the Fourth Congress in 1991, Cuba remained a one-party state committed to the establishment of a socialist society.

Castro used the conclave to again implore the Cuban people to work for *patría*, as he promised to continue the struggle for Cuban independence despite the crumbling of the communist world around him. Castro declared that Cuba would not catch the neoliberal fever that gripped the world's other developing countries. *"Socialismo o muerte"* remained the credo.

Most astonishing to many Cuban watchers was the government's announcement of a papal visit to Cuba in January 1998. After all, the Roman Catholic Church had come under attack early in the revolutionary process. Its schools were closed, foreign nuns and priests expelled, and practicing Catholics harassed by government officials. The state was declared atheistic in 1968 and remained so until 1992. But in the new Cuba of the 1990s small doses of capitalism and Christianity gained official sanction. In December 1997 Christmas became an official holiday again, 31 years after Castro abolished it. Other religions—Protestant, Jewish, and the Afro-Cuban Santeria—also were permitted greater latitude and openness—and perhaps ominously for a political system that had outlawed religion for over a generation, the Cuban youth visibly expressed their religious beliefs.

Fidel Castro's reasons for inviting Pope John Paul II were more important to his foreign policy than to Cuba's domestic situation. Still, the Pope's visit increased the risk of encouraging opposition to the Castro regime. Castro understood that Pope John Paul II's visit to his native Poland in 1979 ushered in a period of political discontent that led to the end of communist rule there. Whereas Polish communist leaders had erred, Castro claimed, the Cuban Revolution had not, and the public confidence he expressed in his own system was bolstered by his call for all Cubans to attend the papal masses. Pope John Paul II's four-day visit, January 21–25, 1998, proved a festive occasion. Large crowds greeted him enthusiastically. His four public masses were well attended, particularly by the Cuban youth. There were only isolated cases of public dissent against the Castro regime. The pontiff, however, did not disappoint those who anticipated his call for change within Cuba. He admonished the lack of family values; criticized government-sanctioned abortion; challenged the youth to serve as the beacon of future progress; chastised the lack of human rights; called for greater political dialogue; and, in a private meeting with Castro, presented a list of political prisoners he wished to be released. Pope John Paul II continued the pressure in a public address at the Vatican after his return from Cuba. He compared this trip to his 1979 visit to Poland.

Castro gambled correctly that the Pope's visit would enhance his image and economy at home. In the weeks immediately following the pontiff's visit, an air of optimism spread over the Cuban populace. There was a greater expression of freedom in the idle gossip at the sidewalk restaurants that dot Havana's busy streets. Castro even promised the release of some 200 political prisoners. But the flurry of optimism quickly faded. In reality, fewer than 100 of the political prisoners were released, and new arrests were made of those who spoke out against the Revolution. And in a decision that surprised none, on February 24, 1998, Cuba's National Assembly elected Fidel Castro as president of the 31-member Council of State for 5 more years and reconfirmed his brother Raúl as First Vice President.

Nor did the Cuban population directly benefit from the estimated $15–$20 million windfall generated by the papal visit through exorbitant hotel, food, and transportation charges, and souvenir buying. The funds went to state-run industries.

Castro also cleverly used the Pope's visit as a vehicle to enhance Cuba's opening in the world community at the expense of the United States. But if Castro was pleased with the Pope's call for an end to the 36-year-old U.S. embargo and his plea for assistance to the poor of Cuba, Castro was not pleased with the U.S. response. Longtime Castro opponent Senator Jesse Helms, with CANF's input, crafted a $100 million federally supported food and medical supply aid program for needy Cubans, possibly using the Roman Catholic Church as the distributor on the island. Promptly, the Clinton administration, several congressmen and senators, and the U.S. Catholic Conference of Bishops blessed the project. Obviously, such a program would empower the Catholic Church and potentially strengthen its position vis-à-vis the regime. Castro understood this, too. He rejected the proposal as a dirty maneuver and rude response to the papal appeal for an end to the U.S. embargo.

Under changing international conditions, the Clinton administration again shifted gears in March 1997, when Secretary of State, Madeline Albright, announced that Cuban exiles could again take direct flights to Havana once a year and send $300 every three months to relatives on the island. Albright also proposed to ease U.S. restrictions and paperwork on the shipment of food and medical supplies to Cuba. But members of the so-called Cuba lobby, such as Helms and Florida Republican congressional representatives Ileana Ros-Lehtinen and Lincoln Díaz-Balart successfully worked to block congressional consideration of the proposal.

Although the United States did not budge, the world community did, again to Castro's satisfaction. The papal visit influenced the Dominican Republic, Guatemala, and Honduras to reestablish diplomatic relations with Cuba by late spring 1998, to be followed later by Argentina and Brazil. Canada, Barbados, and Mexico hinted that they might soon seek Cuba's readmission to the United Nations. Simultaneously, Canadian Prime Minister, Jean Chretien visited Cuba. And in a startling blow to U.S. policy on Cuba, on April 20, 1998, the United Nations Human Rights Commission in Geneva, Switzerland, rejected a U.S. proposal to continue monitoring reported abuses on the island. In Havana, gleeful Cuban officials credited John Paul II's visit in January with helping to bring improvement to Cuba's standing in the international community.

The backlash from the U.S. business community and in the international arena to the Helms-Burton Bill was paralleled by a growing mood

in congress, led by Senators Christopher Dodd (D., Conn.) and John
Warner (R., Va.), and supported by the influential Council on Foreign
Relations and a group of prominent former government leaders (including Henry Kissinger, William Rogers, Frank Carlucci, Howard Baker) that
did not, however, move the Clinton administration. It attempted to mute
the criticism with a number of smaller measures: reinstatement of direct
mail to Cuba; greater number of Miami-Havana charter flights; increase
in the dollar remittances that could be sent to Cuba; and permission to
sell food and medicines to private sector organizations such as religious
groups, privately owned restaurants, and small farmers selling goods in cooperative markets. In February 1999, under the terms of the Torricelli and
Helms-Burton laws, grants were made to bolster and encourage opposition groups in Cuba: Freedom House, Florida International University's
Media Center, and the Cuban Dissident Task Force. Castro interpreted
these actions as examples of continued U.S. interference in his country's
internal affairs.

By 2000, the Helms-Burton Bill limited the president's range of options
that could bring about change in Cuba and end the embargo. Cuban policy had fallen into congressional hands where the Cuba lobby had sufficient power to influence decision-making to control the direction of U.S.
policy.

Castro correctly anticipated that the inauguration of George W. Bush
as the forty-second President of the United States in January 2001 would
further stiffen the U.S. position toward Cuba. Bush came to the White
House with a strong anti-Castro stance. Although he continued Clinton's
suspension of Title III of the Helms-Burton Bill, Bush also described the
40-year-old trade embargo against Cuba as a proper policy tool and a
moral statement and he continued to deny U.S. anchorage to vessels or its
airports to planes that recently visited Cuba. Bush also instructed the
Treasury Department to clamp down on U.S. citizens who traveled to
Cuba without proper documentation with the levying of fines against re-
turnees. And, in the spring of 2002, the administration charged Cuba
with making biochemical weapons, but backed off when critics asserted
otherwise, including former President Jimmy Carter who visited Cuba in
May 2002.

In the international arena, Bush criticized the Mexican government
for its continued Cuban relationship. Under U.S. pressure, Castro was
kept from the Summit of the Americas conference in Quebec, Canada, in
April 2001. The Bush administration also pressured the Mexican government into whisking Castro out of the country following his speech before
the United Nations Financing for Development Conference in Monter-

rey, Mexico, in March 2002 in order to avoid a possible meeting with the late arriving Bush.

Given the tone of the Bush administration, Castro's gestures for rapprochement—purchasing badly needed food supplies following Hurricane Michelle in late 2001, withholding criticism for the housing of terrorist prisoners at the Guantánamo Naval Base, offering to increase cooperation on drug trafficking and terrorism, and signing the 1995 Treaty of Tlatelolco that banned nuclear weapons in the Caribbean and Latin America—failed to impress the administration in Washington.

In his "New Initiative toward Cuba" announced on May 20, 2002, the 100th anniversary of Cuban Independence, Bush raised the bar of preconditions that Castro had to meet before fully realizing the normalization of relations. Diplomatic recognition, open trade, and an aid program will come only when Cuba has a new government that is fully democratic, when the rule of law is respected, and when the human rights of all Cubans are fully protected. Toward those objectives, Bush called upon Castro to permit all political groups to nominate candidates for the 2003 National Assembly, that the vote be by secret ballot, and that it be supervised by international observers. In addition, all political prisoners need to be released and free to participate in those elections, trade unions independent of government control brought into existence, and those workers employed by foreign firms in Cuba should be paid their full salary, not the small percentage permitted by the Cuban government. Bush also announced that his administration would provide aid to nongovernment organizations to be used directly for humanitarian and entrepreneurial activities in Cuba and that the U.S. government would provide scholarships for Cuban students and professionals who want to build civil institutions in Cuba and for family members of political prisoners. Until such a time, the trade embargo remained in effect. The humanitarian proposals continued the U.S. policy of undermining the Castro regime from within.

Retention of the trade embargo brought continued strong opposition. The U.S. business community was joined by Republican congressmen from Midwestern agricultural states who called for a policy change as their constituents saw economic opportunity in Cuba. A bipartisan group of forty congressmen and senators worked throughout 2002 to bring about a change in the embargo policy, but without success. Bush threatened to veto any such legislation. A U.S.-Cuba business conference in February 2002 established the U.S.-Cuba Trade Association. A U.S.-Cuban Trade Show in September 2002 brought representatives from nearly 300 U.S. companies to the island in defiance of the Bush administration policy. The most dramatic change came in November and December 2001 following Hurricane Michelle. Devastated by the storm, Cuba badly needed foodstuffs and U.S. agribusiness—Archer Midland Daniels, Cargill, Riceland, Gold Kist, and Tyson Foods—were quick to fill the gap. Taking advantage of the change in the embargo restrictions in 2000 that permitted the cash sale for foodstuffs, these and other U.S. companies signed deals totaling an estimated $122 million. Castro paid cash from his own treasury and funds borrowed from France.

In the midst of the challenges to Bush's hardline policy, Fidel Castro invited former President Jimmy Carter to visit Cuba. Carter visited the island for four days in May 2002. Carter met with Castro, academics, and dissident groups and was given the green light to visit anywhere in Cuba he wished. The trip made Carter the first former U.S. president to visit Cuba since Calvin Coolidge in 1928 and the most prominent U.S. visitor since Castro came to power in 1959.

The centerpiece of Carter's trip came on May 14 in a 20-minute speech, in Spanish, to the Cuban people on national television. An unedited transcript of the speech appeared in *Granma* on May 16. In it, Carter praised the Cuban government for its educational and health care programs and, while he refrained from criticizing human rights abuses on the island, he criticized the one-party political state and the stifling of opposition. Carter called upon Castro to permit freedom of association and expression, grant individuals the right to own businesses, overhaul the electoral law, and give amnesty to political prisoners. Carter also called upon the United States to take the first step in improving relations by lifting its four-decade-old trade embargo.

Castro remained silent to Carter's admonitions, and President Bush did not take Carter's advice. Three days after Carter's return, on May 20, 2002, the president announced that the trade embargo would remain in place.

The growing domestic and international pressure for the United States to lift its Cuban trade embargo suffered a setback in the spring of 2003 as a result of events within Cuba. In March, the Cuban government henceforth required that the Chief of the U.S. Interests Section in Havana, James Cason, receive government permission to travel outside the capital, where he allegedly encouraged dissident groups to further militate against the Castro regime. That same month, the Cuban government arrested 75 persons—independent journalists, opposition party leaders, human rights advocates, and prodemocracy activists. Subsequently, all received lengthy prison sentences following secret trials. Finally, in early April 2003 three men were executed by a firing squad for their attempt to hijack a Havana harbor ferry to the United States.

The Bush administration responded to the first instance by restricting travel by Cuban diplomats to within the Washington, D.C., Capital Beltway and indicated that travel beyond that point depended upon the Cuban government permitting Cason to travel beyond Havana. In May Bush addressed the second issue with new restrictions on U.S.-Cuban contacts. Henceforth, Treasury licenses would be granted only to independent U.S. organizations that sought to promote democracy in Cuba. So-called humanitarian activities that included construction projects intended "to benefit legitimately independent civil society groups" as well as promote educational training in such fields as civic education, journalism, advocacy, and organizing would receive special consideration. Educational exchanges faced a higher litmus test. While most analysts focused upon the newly-imposed restrictions, little attention was given to the fact that the new rules allowed more Cuban Americans to visit the island and permitted them to carry with them as much as $3,000 in household remittances.

No one doubted that Castro's crackdown in March 2002 emanated from Cuba's declining economy and quality of life, which could trigger another Castro approved exodus like the 1980 Mariel boatlift and the 1994 *balsero* crisis.

In previous economic crises, government crackdowns on dissent were followed by reforms spearheaded by new government appointees who have tended to be younger. Castro repeated that practice in early July 2003 with the appointment of five new loyalists to various government economic posts. They have a mountain to climb. By all estimates, the Cuban economy sank to new depths between 2001 and 2003. Cuba did not escape the drop in world tourism following the terrorist attack on New York City's World Trade Center on September 11, 2001. In the decade preceding the attack, the Cuban government earned about $1 to $1.5 million annually directly from the tourist industry, more than it did from the export of sugar. And the 2003 sugar harvest was lower than that of 2002. The loss of this income translates into a lack of hard currency to purchase goods on the world market. Apparently, Cuba lacked sufficient funds to pay Venezuela for its oil imports. In 2002 alone, oil shipments were interrupted on three occasions as the Venezuelans awaited payment.

The dollarization of the Cuban economy has proved to be a double-edged sword. The dollars come to families with relatives abroad, mostly in the United States, to those who operate tourist restaurants out of their homes, and to the service workers in the tourist industry—maids, bell-hops, taxi drivers, and the like—who are usually tipped in dollars. Exact figures are not available, but estimates of such dollars range from $400 million to $1 billion in the days before September 11, 2001. In turn, these dollars ripple through the economy as payment for the services of skilled artisans such as plumbers, carpenters, electricians, and other repairmen and into the black market for consumer goods, before most of them make their way into the state-owned dollar stores.

But dollarization has created a social problem. The unskilled workers now have more expendable income than highly trained government employees —doctors, lawyers, architects, and teachers. This disparity also has racial overtones. The Cuban professionals are white and account for only 37 percent of the population. The unskilled majority are largely Afro-Cuban.

The government's loss of hard currency has caused other problems for Castro. Since 2001, Cuba's international debt has grown precipitously and its ability to repay has drastically declined. In 2003, Cuba had an estimated $12.2 billion hard currency debt to the Western world and the Cuban government has not paid on it in over a decade. In addition, the Russians want to collect on the $20 billion it advanced Cuba before 1991 and U.S. citizens have approximately $6.3 billion in outstanding expropriation claims. Everyone agrees that Castro cannot pay, and only the wild-eyed optimist thinks that he will collect in the post-Castro era. But for now, Castro has run out of creditors.

The government's lack of income means that it cannot provide adequate services to the people. Based upon data gathered from *Granma*, in 2002 at least 13 percent of the population was clinically undernourished, and the state's food rationing system provides for only a week to 10 days of basic nutritional needs each month. Although the government claims that unemployment stood at 3.3 percent, outside observers put the figure at 30 percent. An important sign of Cuba's desperation was the 40 percent jump in food imports from the United States during the first quarter of 2003.

The foreign visitor to Havana may not see beyond the revitalized "Old Havana," or the United Nations financed reconstruction of the stately old homes along Havana's waterfront *Malecón*, or the tourist hotels and government buildings. But if the tourist ventures only several blocks beyond the glitter, he would find that Cuban life is very difficult. Housing, education, and health care are free, but the buildings are collapsing, the schools don't have enough books, and medicine is often in short supply, just as food rations are. Public transportation is cheap, but the service is abysmal. Large trucks, called camels because of their unusual high-backed shape, carry people around Havana's suburbs like sardines in a can. Elsewhere, people either trudge through the humidity, ride bicycles, or ride on the backs of trucks. But, as in the past, the average Cuban's life pales by comparison to the lifestyle of the elite Communist Party members.

Cuba has the makings of a powder keg ready to explode. Castro admitted as much in a wide-ranging interview with ABC-TV newsperson Barbara Walters on October 11, 2002. Still, he audaciously told Walters that "socialism works in our country [Cuba]." He also made it clear that he is still in control of Cuba, despite the Varilla Project, in which over 11,000 Cubans petitioned for greater democracy in the country. Castro admitted their constitutional right to petition the government, but he doubted that the National Assembly would change existing governmental processes.

Castro continues to cling to power propped by a military that directly controls about 60 percent of the national economy. Apparently secure in his position, Castro told the Cuban people on July 29, 2003, the fiftieth anniversary of the Moncada assault, that Cuba has proven to the world that "socialism is capable of achieving a society that is a thousand times fairer and more humane" than the world's so-called advanced capitalist nations.

In 2003, Castro's Revolution appeared to have come full circle from 1963 when he took the island down the socialist path. The economy is in chaos, the quality of life is miserable, and political repression and U.S. pressure are on the increase.

Chapter 6

CONCLUSION

Fidel Castro arrived in Havana on January 1, 1959, determined to take control of the Cuban Revolution. Nothing in his past—his childhood and early schooling in eastern Cuba, his days at Belén High School and the University of Havana, or his early political career—suggested otherwise. Over the years Castro resisted joining organizations that demanded loyalty to its credo. Instead he became increasingly independent of others and used them only to serve his own purposes. For the same reasons, groups rejected Castro. His affiliation with the *Ortodoxo* Party and relationship with the Communist Party before 1953 illustrate the point. As the Revolution turned violent in 1953, the anti-Batista forces that gathered in Montreal, Canada, in June 1953 did not invite Castro to participate, and his joining the Caracas Pact in July 1958 was a pragmatic decision to be jettisoned when necessary. Thus, when he arrived in Havana, Castro was determined to eliminate all sources of potential opposition: the *Batistianos*; the landed elite, both native and foreign; individuals like Hubert Matos and Anibal Escalante; and the Communist Party leadership. He did so, and by 1964 Castro was the effective head of government, propped by his revolutionary army.

The institutionalization of the Revolution, with the strengthening of the newly organized PCC and the 1976 constitution, confirmed Castro's centrality. He became head of both the party and government. He presides over the party's Central Committee that sets the action agenda. According to the 1976 constitution, as President of the Council of State, Castro is automatically the head of state and government. Effectively, he controls the legislative agenda, decides on government appointments, and approves candidates for the various assemblies. Only the most loyal, who pledge themselves to carry out the government's programs, are selected. The constitution requires the defense of the Revolution and it leaves no room for dissent. This is reinforced by the mass organizations—the CDRs, FMC, ANAP, and the CTC. All are charged with insuring the implementation of the Revolution. Effectively, Castro sets the Revolution's agenda and deviation from it is not tolerated. Literally, Fidel Castro is the Maximum Leader, a fact confirmed by the Communist Party Congresses in 1986, 1991, and 1997.

When Castro declared that he was a Marxist-Leninist in December 1961, it was based upon the pragmatic need for economic assistance. He came to Havana two years earlier as an idealistic socialist, not with a definite plan to implement a socialistic or Marxist society. He failed to take into account the consequences of his 1959 Agrarian Reform Law and Urban Reform Law or the squandering away of the treasury surplus left behind by Fulgencio Batista. His confrontation with the United States that resulted in the nationalization of U.S.-owned industries in Cuba satisfied Cuban nationalism, but nowhere did he consider its adverse impact upon the Cuban economy.

Starting in late 1959, Castro was too busy chastising the Cubans who went into exile to realize that he was losing Cuba's most talented workers. Castro's idealism permitted him to accept Che Guevara's notion that workers would produce for the good of the Revolution, rather than monetary rewards. Nor did Castro demonstrate much foresight when he pushed for a ten-million-ton sugar crop in 1970, which had a devastating effect upon the remainder of Cuba's economy. These actions indicate a naive and irresponsible leader, not one committed to a plan for a Marxist-Leninist society.

In 1970, Castro turned to Soviet-style centralized planning as a precondition for badly needed assistance from Moscow. But with his Rectification Program in 1986, Castro jettisoned many of the Soviet practices, including the SDPE that contributed to Cuba's economic stagnation. Until the collapse of the Soviet Union in 1991, Castro directed tighter control over the economy and again exhorted the Cuban people to work and produce for the good of the Revolution. Ever the pragmatist, Castro again shifted economic gears following the Soviet collapse to permit petit capitalists to operate throughout Cuba and for the government to engage in joint ventures with foreign companies in the development of the Cuban economy. At the start of the twenty-first century, however, the Cuban economy was on a downward spiral. Foodstuffs and consumer goods were in short supply. Housing and basic services, such as telephone, electricity, and mass transit, were in disarray. Still, Castro remained committed to the Revolution. *"Socialismo o Muerte,"* he told the Cuban people.

Castro came to Havana in January 1959 as an avowed anti-American Cuban nationalist. He made his point with the nationalization of U.S. industries and his public tirades against the United States, in and outside of Cuba. Given the Cold War atmosphere of the day, Castro naively thought that the Soviet Union would defend this island outpost of socialism only 90 miles from the United States. After all, the United States was the avowed enemy of both the Cubans and Soviets, Castro reasoned. He discovered otherwise during the 1962 missile crisis when the two superpowers settled the problem themselves, without consulting with Castro upon whose soil the Soviet missiles sat.

Following the Soviet economic commitment to Cuba after 1970, Castro adjusted his thinking. Castro now concluded that the Soviets could not afford to abandon him or his Revolution without risking damage to its image elsewhere in the developing world and, possibly, a challenge from its Eastern European satellites. This confidence enabled Castro to venture into the world, first with humanitarian assistance given by doctors, teachers, technicians, and the like. It earned him much good will and significantly contributed to his being elected President of the Non-Aligned Movement in 1979. The relative stability of the Cuban economy and higher prices for sugar in the world market enabled Castro to establish beneficial relationships with countries in Western Europe, Latin America, and Japan, all against the wishes of U.S. policy. But it was Castro's military adventures into Africa, Grenada, and Central America that earned him the wrath of the United States, particularly from the Reagan and Bush administrations.

In the 1980s, as the United States tightened its embargo on Cuba and increased the political pressure upon Castro, the Soviet Union was beginning to unravel. With its collapse in 1991, the Cubans lost their economic benefactor, which, in turn, curbed Castro's international adventurism. As the new century dawned in 2001, Castro cast about for new supporters.

In many ways the Revolution has come full circle between 1959 and 2003. As Castro's policies ruined the Cuban economy in a few years after 1959, the same was true for post-1991. As he had exchanged U.S. economic dependency for a similar relationship with the Soviet Union, he now casts about for a nation or group of nations to bail out his floundering economy. As he eliminated political opposition in the 1960s and exhorted the Cuban people to commit themselves to the Revolution, he does so again in the years after 1991. And as he did through the 1960s,

Castro again confronts a United States determined to strangle his Revolution to death.

At age 76, Castro cannot go on forever, but who will replace him is pure conjecture. Fidel anointed his brother Raúl as the heir apparent, but this ignores Fidel's closest advisors and the military officers who themselves may want power. One must also consider the new generation of communist loyalists just now making their way into the party and government apparatus. One group that *can* be discounted are the Cuban Americans, now two generations removed from Cuba. Although vociferous and apparently influential in the making of U.S. policy, they are too well entrenched in the United States to start over again in Cuba. And, if they do return, the Cubans who have endured two generations of economic deprivation and political repression will not welcome their brethren home. Their pragmatic interests in such things as housing, health care, education, transportation, and the like must be served by whomever follows Fidel Castro.

FURTHER READING

Fidel Castro, Biographies

Balfour, Sebastian. *Castro*. London: Longman, 1995.
    A brief biography of Castro with little analysis.

Bourne, Peter G. *Fidel: A Biography of Fidel Castro*. New York: Dodd, Mead, 1986.
    Emphasizes Castro's psychological characteristics that motivated him.

Dubois, Jules. *Fidel Castro: Rebel-Liberator or Dictator*. Indianapolis, Ind.: Bobbs-Merrill, 1959.
    An unequivocal defense of Castro by a French socialist.

Beto, Frei. *Fidel and Religion*. New York: Simon and Schuster, 1987.
    A discussion with Fidel Castro about his childhood and views on religion.

Franqui, Carlos. *Family Portrait with Fidel*. New York: Random House, 1983.
    A critical assessment of Fidel by one of his closest advisors.

Geyer, Georgie Anne. *Guerrilla Prince: The Untold Story of Fidel Castro*. Boston, Mass.: Little, Brown, 1991.
    Focuses on the personal aspects of Castro's life.

Halperin, Maurice. *The Rise and Decline of Fidel Castro*. Berkeley: University of California Press, 1972.
    One of the earlier critical analyses of Castro and his political intentions for Cuba.

Liss, Sheldon B. *Fidel! Castro's Political and Social Thought*. Boulder, Colo.: Westview Press, 1994.
    An intellectual biography of Castro.

Mathews, Herbert. *Fidel Castro*. New York: Random House, 1969.
    Provides a sympathetic political biography.

Quirk, Robert. *Fidel Castro*. New York: W.W. Norton, 1993.
>   A particularly rich treatment of the early years of the Revolution through 1968.
Szulc, Tad. *Fidel: A Critical Portrait*. New York: William Morrow and Co., 1986. Completed with the collaboration of Cuban officials, including Castro. This is one of the most detailed studies about Castro.

Fidel Castro, Writings

Castro, Fidel. *Building Socialism in Cuba, 1960–1962*. New York: Pathfinder Press, 1985.
>   A vast collection of speeches that trace Cuba's transition to a socialist state.
———. *Cuba's International and Foreign Policy, 1975–1980*, 3rd ed. New York: Pathfinder Press, 1981.
>   Castro speaks out on events in Grenada, Nicaragua, and Africa and on relations with the United States.
———. *History Will Absolve Me*. New York: The Viking Press, 1968.
>   Castro's defense at the Moncada trial in 1953.
———. *In Defense of Socialism, 1988–1989*. New York: Pathfinder Press, 1989.
>   This collection deals with the crucial years in which Castro attempts to reignite a revolutionary zeal among the Cuban people while facing the loss of Soviet support.
———. *Fidel: My Early Years*. Melbourne: Ocean Press, 1998.
>   Castro reflects on his youth through the preparations for the 1953 attack upon the Moncada barracks.
———. *Revolutionary Struggle, 1947–1958*. Cambridge, Mass.: MIT Press, 1972.
>   A collection of articles and speeches up to the triumph of the Revolution.
Kenner, Martin, and James Petras, eds. *Fidel Castro Speaks*. New York: Grove Press, 1969.
>   A collection of speeches that focuses on the pitfalls of capitalism in Latin America and Cuba's effort to correct them through communism.

Other Revolutionary Participants

Anderson, Jon Lee. *Che Guevara: A Revolutionary Life*. New York: Grove Press, 1996.
>   A reporter who interviewed several of Guevara's colleagues and examined not previously seen Cuban documents, Anderson concludes that Guevara was an idealistic revolutionary.

Batista, Fulgencio. *Cuba Betrayed*. New York: Random House, 1962.
> A defense of his own regime which includes criticisms of the United States for letting Cuba fall to Castro.

Castañeda, Jorge. *Compañero: The Life and Death of Che Guevara*. New York: Alfred A. Knopf, 1997.
> A thoughtful and scholarly reassessment of Guevara as one who was taken in by the ideals of Marxism-Leninism.

Franqui, Carlos. *Diary of the Cuban Revolution*. New York: Viking Press, 1980.
> An invaluable collection of letters and documents of the Sierra campaign by one of Castro's closest aides who later was denounced by the Maximum Leader.

Guevara, Ernesto Che. *Reminiscences of the Cuban Revolutionary War*. New York: Pathfinder, 1969.
> Castro's chief lieutenant provides insight into the leadership and strategies of the revolutionary movement.

Llerena, Mario. *The Unsuspected Revolution: The Birth and Rise of Castroism*. Ithaca, N.Y.: Cornell University Press, 1978.
> A memoir of the anti-Batista struggle by an early supporter and later opponent of Fidel Castro.

Macaulay, Neill. *A Rebel in Cuba: An American's Memoir*. Chicago, Ill.: Quadrangle Books, 1970.
> Account of a young idealist at the time who fought with Castro, only to leave the island as the revolution radicalized.

Phillips, R. Hart. *Cuba, Island of Paradox*. New York: McDowell, Obolensky, 1959.
> This *New York Times* reporter provides a perceptive first-person account of Cuba from the early 1930s to Castro's triumph in 1959.

Urrutia Lleo, Manuel. *Fidel Castro and Company, Inc*. New York: Praeger, 1984.
> Cuba's first post-Batista president finds Castro and his cohorts deliberately putting Cuba on the path to communism.

Cuba and the Revolution Since 1959

del Aguila, Juan M. *Cuba: Dilemmas of a Revolution*. Boulder, Colo.: Westview Press, 1984.
> A brief examination of the economic, social, and political changes brought to Cuba during the first 25 years of the revolution.

Azicri, Max. *Cuba: Politics, Economics, and Society*. London: Pinter Publishers, 1988.
> An examination of the role that education, cinema, poetry, music, and theater had during the revolutionary years.

Baloyra, Enrique A., and James A. Morris, eds. *Conflict and Change in Cuba.* Albuquerque: University of New Mexico Press, 1993.

A collection of essays dealing with the traditions of the revolution and the reality of the changing world.

Bengelsdorf, Carrolle. *The Problem of Democracy in Cuba: Between Vision and Reality.* New York: Oxford University Press, 1994.

An examination of the deepening crisis in Cuba against the larger backdrop of *perestroika* and the collapse of socialism in Eastern Europe.

Bunck, Julie Marie. *Fidel Castro and the Quest for a Revolutionary Culture in Cuba.* University Park: Pennsylvania State University Press, 1994.

Bunck examines Castro's effort to incorporate children, women, labor, and sports into the revolutionary process.

Butterworth, Douglas. *The People of Buena Ventura: Relocation of Slum Dwellers in Post-Revolutionary Cuba.* Urbana: University of Illinois Press, 1980.

An ethnographic study of a working-class community in Havana.

Draper, Theodore. *Castroism: Theory and Practice.* New York: Praeger, 1965.

An early monograph that frames the passionate debate in defense of Castro's revolution.

Eckstein, Susan E. *Back from the Future: Cuba under Castro.* Princeton, N.J.: Princeton University Press, 1994.

A most cogent analysis of the revolution's thirty-five years and the crisis it confronted.

Fabrico, Roberto. *The Winds of December.* East Rutherford, N.J.: Fairleigh Dickinson University Press, 1980.

The most complete and most comprehensive account of the final months of the armed struggle against Batista.

Fagen, Richard R. *The Transformation of Political Culture in Cuba.* Stanford, Calif.: Hoover Institution Press, 1969.

An important study that focuses on the 1961 literacy campaign, schools of revolutionary instruction and the establishment of the Committees for the Defense of the Revolution.

Feinsilver, Julie M. *Healing the Masses: Cuban Health Politics at Home and Abroad.* Berkeley: University of California Press, 1993.

A thorough examination of medical policies and healthcare systems in Cuba after the revolution.

Figueroa Esteva, Max. *The Basic Secondary School in the Country: An Education Innovation in Cuba.* Paris: UNESCO Press, 1974.

An examination of the secondary rural school programs.

García, María Cristina. *Havana USA: Cuban Exiles and Cuban Americans in South Florida, 1959–1994.* Berkeley: University of California Press, 1996.

The first major synthesis of the Cuban-American community in south Florida.

Karol, K. S. *Guerrillas in Power: The Course of the Cuban Revolution*. New York: Hill and Wang, 1970.

A detailed discussion of the antecedents of the revolution through Castro's failed economic policies of 1970.

Kirk, John M. *Between God and the Party: Religion and Politics in Revolutionary Cuba*. Gainesville: University Presses of Florida, 1989.

This volume is considered the seminal work on relations between the Catholic church and the revolutionary government.

Lewis, Oscar, Ruth M. Lewis, and Susan M. Rigdon. *Four Men Living a Revolution: An Oral History of Contemporary Cuba*. Urbana: University of Illinois Press, 1978.

Presents oral histories of men and women, old and young, black and white all living in a Havana apartment.

———. *Four Women Living the Revolution: An Oral History of Contemporary Cuba*. Urbana: University of Illinois Press, 1977.

Lengthy interviews with a single woman and former counterrevolutionary, an educated married woman and member of the Communist Party, a domestic servant, and a prostitute.

Masud-Piloto, Felix. *From Welcome Exiles to Illegal Immigrants: Cuban Migration to the U.S., 1959–1995*. Lanham, Md.: Rowman & Littlefield, 1996.

A brief study of the changing character of the Cubans migrating to the United States since the revolution and U.S. policy regarding them.

Matthews, Herbert. *The Cuban Story*. New York: G. Brazilier, 1961.

A sympathetic account of the Cuban Revolution by a *New York Times* reporter.

Mesa-Lago, Carmelo. *The Economy of Socialist Cuba: A Two Decade Appraisal*. Albuquerque: University of New Mexico Press, 1981.

A critical assessment of the Cuban economy through the late 1970s.

Pérez-López, Jorge F. *Cuba at a Crossroads: Politics and Economics after the Fourth Party Congress*. Gainesville: University Presses of Florida, 1994.

An analysis of the issues confronting the First Communist Party Congress meeting in Cuba following the loss of Soviet assistance.

Pérez-Stable, Marifeli. *The Cuban Revolution: Origins, Course, and Legacy*. New York: Oxford University Press, 1993.

A sympathetic, yet excellent analysis of the course of the Revolution.

Pflaum, Irving P. *Tragic Island: How Communism Came to Cuba*. Englewood Cliffs, N.J.: Prentice Hall, 1961.

A critical analysis that focuses on Castro's betrayal of the ideals of those who fought with him to oust Batista.

Short, Margaret I. *Law and Religion in Marxist Cuba*. New Brunswick, N.J.: Transaction Books, 1993.

A critical evaluation of religious freedom within the larger context of human rights conditions.

Stubbs, Jean. *Cuba: The Test of Time*. London: Latin American Bureau, 1989.

A brief and positive interpretation about the accomplishments of the Cuban revolution.

Suchlicki, Jaimie, ed. *The Cuban Military under Castro*. Miami, Fla.: Institute for Inter-American Studies, University of Miami, 1989.

A number of informative essays about the development of the military under Castro.

Suárez, Andrés. *Cuba: Castroism and Communism*. Cambridge, Mass.: MIT Press, 1967.

An early, but significant discussion of the radicalization of the revolution and its path to socialism.

Cuba and World Affairs

Benjamin, Jules. *The United States and the Origins of the Cuban Revolution*. Princeton, N.J.: Princeton University Press, 1990.

Emphasizes the critical decades before the revolution.

Blight, James G., Bruce J. Allen, and David A. Welch. *Cuba on the Brink: Castro, the Missile Crisis, and the Soviet Collapse*. New York: Pantheon Books, 1993.

Despite its title, the volume focuses on the 1962 missile crisis with transcripts from a Havana conference on the subject that included such key players as Castro and Robert McNamara.

Bonsal, Philip W. *Cuba, Castro, and the United States*. Pittsburgh, Pa.: University of Pittsburgh Press, 1971.

An account of Cuban-American relations by the U.S. Ambassador in Havana from 1959 until the embassy's closing in January 1961.

Brenner, Philip. *From Confrontation to Negotiation: U.S. Relations with Cuba*. Boulder, Colo.: Westview Press, 1988.

This brief book focuses upon the 1980s and provides an excellent outline of the U.S. and Cuban positions on issues affecting their bilateral relations.

Conde, Yvonne M. *Operation Pedro Pan: The Untold Exodus of 14,048 Cuban Children*. New York: Routledge, 1999.

An excellent discussion of the program that brought Cuban children to the United States immediately after the Cuban Revolution, including their lives into the contemporary.

Congressional Research Service. *Cuba: Background and Current Issues for Congress*. Washington, D.C.: Congressional Research Service, 2001.

Prepared by the Latin American specialists of the CRS, the report provides an excellent understanding of the issues affecting U.S.-Cuban relations at the beginning of the George W. Bush presidency.

Council on Foreign Relations. *U.S.-Cuban Relations in the 21st Century.* New York: Council on Foreign Relations, 2002.

A bipartisan task force recommends greater contacts between the Cuban American community in the United States and other Americans and NGOs with people and groups on the island of Cuba. Its recommendations contrast sharply with the policies pursued by the George W. Bush administration.

Domínguez, Jorge I. *To Make a World Safe for Revolution: Cuba's Foreign Policy.* Cambridge, Mass.: Harvard University Press, 1989.

An examination of Fidel Castro's foreign policy, demonstrating both its defensive character to secure the island and to capitalize upon civil discontent in the Third World.

Duncan, W. Raymond. *The Soviet Union and Cuba: Interests and Influence.* New York: Praeger, 1985.

A comprehensive analysis of relations between Moscow and Havana.

Erisman, H. Michael. *Cuba's International Relations: The Anatomy of a Nationalistic Foreign Policy.* Boulder, Colo.: Westview Press, 1985.

An excellent brief account and analysis of Castro's foreign policy for the first 25 years of the revolution.

———. *Cuba's Foreign Relations in a Post-Soviet World.* Gainesville: University Press of Florida, 2000.

Erisman supplements the material from his early study on Cuban foreign policy to include policy after 1991.

Falk, Pamela. *Cuban Foreign Policy: Caribbean Tempest.* Lexington, Mass.: D.C. Heath, 1986.

Contends that Castro pursued a foreign policy independent of the Soviet Union.

Gleijeses, Piero. *Conflicting Missions: Havana, Washington, and Africa, 1959–1976.* Chapel Hill: University of North Carolina Press, 2002.

An exhaustive and scholarly analysis of the conflicting policies of the United States and Cuba regarding the latter's interests in Africa.

Kaplowitz, Donna Rich. *Anatomy of a Failed Embargo: U.S. Sanctions against Cuba.* Boulder, Colo.: Lynne Rienner Publishers, 1998.

A brief analytical volume providing insights into the failure of U.S. policy, even through the most recent times.

———, ed. *Cuba's Ties to a Changing World.* Boulder, Colo.: Lynne Rienner Publishers, 1993.

An important collection of essays that presents various perspectives on Cuba's relations with the world following the collapse of the Soviet Union.

Levine, Barry, ed. *The New Cuban Presence in the Caribbean.* Boulder, Colo.: Westview Press, 1983.

An important collection of essays regarding Cuba's initiatives in the late 1970s and early 1980s in the Caribbean and Central America.

Morley, Morris H. *Imperial State: The United States and Revolutionary Cuba, 1952–1986.* London: Cambridge University Press, 1986.

An Australian political scientist, Morley argues that U.S. hostility toward the revolution prevents accommodation between Washington and Havana.

Paterson, Thomas G. *Contesting Castro: The United States and the Triumph of the Cuban Revolution.* New York: Oxford University Press, 1994.

Focuses upon President John F. Kennedy's determination to topple Castro from power.

Pavlov, Yuri. *Soviet-Cuban Alliance, 1959–1991.* Coral Gables, Fla.: North-South Center Press, 1994.

The Soviet mistrust of Fidel Castro is the theme pursued by this former Soviet diplomat.

Smith, Earl E. T. *The Fourth Floor: An Account of the Castro Communist Revolution.* New York: Random House, 1962.

The former U.S. Ambassador to Havana recalls the last two years of the Batista regime.

Smith, Wayne. *Closest of Enemies: A Personal and Diplomatic Account of U.S.-Cuba Relations Since 1957.* New York: W.W. Norton, 1987.

A personal and critical account of U.S. policy toward revolutionary Cuba by the former head of the U.S. Interests Section in Havana.

Turner, William W. *The Fish Is Red: The Story of the Secret War Against Castro.* New York: Harper and Row, 1981.

A study of the U.S. covert operations against Castro and Cuba during the 1960s and 1970s.

Welch, Richard E., Jr. *Response to Revolution: The United States and Cuban Revolution, 1959–1961.* Chapel Hill: University of North Carolina Press, 1985.

An excellent scholarly analysis of Washington's response to the evolving revolutionary process in Cuba.

Wright, Thomas C. *Latin America in the Era of the Cuban Revolution.* New York: Praeger, 1991.

An examination of the impact of Castro's revolution upon the various communist movements across Latin America.

Wyden, Peter. *The Bay of Pigs Story.* New York: Simon & Schuster, 1979.

Provides a standard account of the invasion, especially its planning and execution.

Audio Visual Materials

20th Century with Mike Wallace: Cuba and Castro. 60-minute video, A&E Television, 1998.

An examination of Cuba since 1959 and the dominant place Fidel Castro has in it.

The Bay of Pigs. 57-minute video, PBS, 1997.

Combines footage and interviews to explore the event and the long-term effects it has had upon the two countries.

Bay of Pigs Declassified. 50-minute video, A&ME Home Entertainment, 2000.

Drawing upon recently released documentation, scholars analyze the ill-fated invasion, its place in the Cold War and how it continues to color U.S.-Cuban relations.

Covering Cuba. 114-minute video, AB Independent Productions, 1995.

Examines the realities of living in Cuba before and after the Revolution, as contrasted with the vastly different portrayal of Cuba and Fidel Castro in the United States media.

Cuba. 25-minute video, National Geographic Society, 1990.

Discusses the transformation under Castro, showing improvements in education and health care as well as problems with housing and transportation.

Cuba: A Portrait. 60-minute video, World's Together, 2001.

Takes the viewer across Cuba from Havana to *Isla de Juventude* in the south and Baracoa in the far west.

Cuba: The Children of Fidel. 60-minute video, Films for the Humanities, 1998.

This program examines the lives of 13 Cuban women, representing a cross section of Cuban society, and their experiences of living in Castro's Cuba.

Cuba at the Crossroads: The Roots of the Revolution. 35-minute video, Cinema Guild, 1999.

An American filmmaker travels throughout Cuba examining the current social and economic realities experienced by the average citizen of Cuba.

Cuba va: The Challenge of the Next Generation. 57-minute video, Cuba Video Project, 1993.

Considers Cuba's future from the perspective of Cuba's youth as they discuss the economic crisis of the early 1990s and the need for change.

The Cuban Excludables. 57-minute video, Richter Productions, 1994.

Depicts the plight of the detainees and the human rights abuses they suffered after the 1980 Mariel Boatlift.

Fidel Castro: Betrayed Hope. 50-minute video, Home Vision Entertainment, 2000.

Demonstrates Fidel Castro's charisma that has kept him in power for 40 years.

Fidel Castro: Big Man, Small Island. 50-minute video, Films for the Humanities, 2001.

A biography of Fidel Castro from his school days to the present time.

Greener Grass: Cuba, Baseball, and the United States. 60-minute video, PBS, 2000.
 Documents how the two countries have used baseball as a political tool and how the sport has operated both as a bridge and barrier between the two lands.

Last Days of the Revolution. 60-minute video, PBS, 1994.
 Illustrates the hardships of the Cuban people during the "Special Period," and examines the impact of the U.S. embargo and the shift in U.S. immigration policy.

A New Cuban Crisis. 37-minute video, Filmmakers Library, 1998.
 A presentation about the 1996 shooting of two Brothers to the Rescue planes allegedly in Cuban waters. Includes international reaction to the incident.

La Otra Cuba (The Other Cuba). 94-minute video, Connoisseur Meridian Films, 1998.
 Recounts Cuba's political history from Fulgencio Batista's 1952 coup d' état to the 1980 Mariel exodus.

Portrait of Castro's Cuba. 91-minute video, Ambrose Video, 1991.
 Actor James Earl Jones explores Cuba as it has become under Fidel Castro.

Saving Elían. 60-minute video, PBS, 2001.
 Documentary report about the five-year-old Cuban boy rescued from the waters off Florida's coast in 2000 who became the focus of a struggle between Cuba and the United States and within the Cuban American community.

The Uncompromising Revolution. 80-minute video, Telemation, 1989.
 Provides a brief history of Cuba and then discusses the nationalization of American businesses, Soviet aid and weapons, and Cuba's role in Latin America, Africa, and Central America.

Voices of Cuba. 54-minute video, Landmark Video, 2001.
 Examines the lives of Cubans from ghetto residents to the privileged Communist elite. The people speak about the Revolution, the effects of the U.S. embargo, and the hopes for their country in the twenty-first century.

Internet Sites for Contemporary Cuba

Cuban American National Foundation (CANF). http://www.canfnet.org.
 The official news site of the CANF. Contains news stories, and commentary, and directs readers to its reports about Cuba.

Center for International Policy—Cuba Project. http://www.ciponline.org/cuba new/.
 A Washington, D.C., research center. Its Cuba project is critical of U.S. policy toward Cuba. The site offers position papers and analysis of U.S. policy.

CIA Factbook. http://www.odci.gov/publications/factbook/geus/us/html.
    A reference source that provides encyclopedic information about Cuba's
    geography, government, transportation, and military.
Cuba Policy Foundation. http://www.cubafoundation.org.
    An organization of senior diplomats in former Republican Party adminis-
    trations opposed to trade embargo on Cuba. It is consulted often by the
    communications media. Its Web site contains position statements.
Department of State—Office of International Information Program, United
    States and Cuba. http://www.usinfo/state.gov/regional/ar/US-Cuba.
    Provides a collection of documents, position papers, and official state-
    ments on current U.S. policy toward Cuba.
Department of State: The United States and Cuba. http://www.state.gov/www/
    regions/wha/cuba/.
    This site serves as a permanent archive of official information related to
    U.S.-Cuban relations released prior to June 20, 2001.
Granma International. http://www.granma.cu/ingles/index.html.
    Granma is Cuba's official newspaper and, as such, presents news, commen-
    tary, and opinion as reflected by the Cuban government.
Havana Home Page. http://citease.netspacetoday.com/havana/.
    The official site for the U.S. Interests Section located in the Embassy of
    Switzerland, Havana, Cuba. In addition to describing its functions, the
    site provides information regarding current U.S.-Cuban relations.
Online News Service. http://www.pbs.org/newshow/bb/latin_america/cuba.
    Provides a summary of recent events in U.S.-Cuban relations
United States-Cuba Relations. http://www.rose-hulman.edu/m/dellacova/U.S.-
    Cuba.html.
    Provides photos, news clippings, and articles on U.S.-Cuban relations
    since 1998.

INDEX

About the Author

THOMAS M. LEONARD is Professor of History at the University of North Florida.